FIELD OF SPEARS

THE LAST MISSION OF THE JORDAN CREW

*

GREGORY HADLEY

WITH A FOREWORD BY

PHILIP SEATON

FIELD OF SPEARS

First published by Paulownia Press 2007

www.paulowniapress.co.uk

ISBN 978-0-9555582-1-4 (Paperback)

British Library Cataloguing in Publication Data
A catalogue record for this book is available from the British Library

Gregory Hadley has asserted his
moral right to be identified as
the author of this work.

Printed in the UK by
Biddles Ltd.
24 Rollesby Road, Hardwick Industrial Estate,
King's Lynn, Norfolk PE30 4LS

Paulownia Press Limited
A Private Limited Company registered in the UK
Company Registration No: 05992165

Dedicated to those who made it back alive,

but never survived the war.

TABLE OF CONTENTS

ACKNOWLEDGEMENTS

I wish to express my heartfelt gratitude to the following people and organizations for their permission to use historical documents, personal photographs, diaries and personal letters, all of which have made it possible to preserve the memory of the incidents recorded in this book. Any errors, confusion or significant omissions, however, are entirely my fault and responsibility. I also wish to thank those below who offered help in translating difficult Japanese documents and for helping to open doors that would have otherwise been closed to me. Finally, my special thanks to Niigata University of International and Information Studies, which provided a grant for the publication of this book.

Kenneth Cambon, Marie Cambon, Ray Chatwin, Howard Chittenden, William Conine, Phil Crowther, Gregory Dunne, Thomas Feaster, Motoichi Fujita, Toru Fukubayashi, Hitoshi Fukuda, Milton Garin, Harry George, Robert Grant, Sue Kay Grant, The Honorable Robert T. Groh (Ret.), Hiromi Hadley, Ronald Hadley, Raymond 'Hap' Halloran, Fiske Hanley, Dr. Nicholas Henck, Asako Horiuchi, Wes Injerd, David Jeffrey, Paul Keenan, Koshi Kobayashi, Jay Martin, George and Mary McGraw, Virgil Morgan, Toshio Ochi, James Oglethorpe, Joseph Papalia, John Powers, The POW Research Group of Japan, The 6th Bomb Group Association, Reuters/ITN, Dr. Charles Roland, Tadashi Saito, Hikaru Sato, Dr. Philip Seaton, Jerry Spero, Dr. Michael Steiner, Mark Stevens, Justin Taylan, Paul Tibbits, Hidemasa Tomii, Andrew Trump, John Trump, Paul Trump, Toshihide Uemura, Patricia Wadley, Masao Watanabe, Toshio Watanabe, William B. Webster III, Dr. Greg Wilsbacher.

FOREWORD

People who have never been to Japan can be forgiven for having never heard of Niigata. It is a largely rural prefecture facing the Japan Sea about 300 km north-northeast of Tokyo. The prefectural capital, Niigata City, is a bustling regional centre of around 500,000 that has expanded by mergers with neighbouring towns to over 800,000 in 2005. Although it is a major port city, life continues at a gentle pace. During my three years living and working in Nagaoka, the prefecture's second city, I was frequently told that the water, rice, *sake* and the annual fireworks display were the best reasons for living there. The area contains some of the most expansive agricultural plains in Japan, where the nationally famous *koshihikari* rice is cultivated using melt water from the Japan Alps and the region's plentiful precipitation.

Niigata has been made much more accessible to Tokyo since the opening of the Jōetsu *shinkansen* (bullet train) in 1982, but the prefecture as a whole is a quiet part of Japan and does not feature particularly prominently in national, let alone international news. In October 2004, it briefly became the spotlight of international attention after a devastating earthquake. Niigata's other main claims to international fame in the modern era are as one of the venues for the 2002 FIFA World Cup and as the home prefecture of maverick politician Kakuei Tanaka, the prime minister in the 1970s who restored relations with China but fell from grace (although not influence) after the Lockheed Scandal of 1976.

Niigata's role in the history of World War II is obscure even within Japan. Niigata City's port was a vital gateway to China, Korea and Manchuria. The war exhibits at the Niigata Prefectural Museum of History in Nagaoka focus on three aspects of the war: the air raid on Nagaoka on 1 August 1945 that killed over 1,400 people, the emigration of settlers to Manchuria, and the slave labor of around 3,000 Allied POWs in the prefecture's prison camps. The other notable war role of the prefecture was that Admiral Isoroku Yamamoto, the architect of the Pearl Harbor attack, was born in Nagaoka. However, Niigata City is most famous for what did *not* happen there: It was one of the cities originally identified as a potential A-bomb target, fates that were suffered instead by Hiroshima and Nagasaki.

Niigata, therefore, would not be the first part of Japan to come to mind for a book about air raids and the fate of a downed B-29 crew. Other cities suffered much larger casualties in air raids, and the most infamous vengeance meted out on downed B-29 crews was the vivisections carried out at Kyushu Imperial University. But *Field of Spears* is not simply another book about air raids or the treatment of downed B-29ers by their Japanese captors. It is first and foremost a study of local history and of the history of ordinary individuals brought together by their roles in a brutal world war.

The importance of local history in Japan cannot be underestimated. Regional identities are very strong: for example, the Japan Alps constitute a considerable geographical, climatic and cultural barrier between Niigata and Tokyo, which lies on the Kanto Plain. In addition, local identities and history are particularly important in the context of contemporary Japanese war discourses. Given the discomfort and contestation that ensues from using a national frame to remember a war of aggression that killed over 20 million people throughout Asia, history is frequently narrated at the local level, particularly of local victim-hood in air raids or in the loss of regional battalions. The national commemorations that continue to stir anger and controversy throughout Asia, such as prime ministerial worship at Yasukuni Shrine, which memorializes Japan's military dead, are only one layer of remembrance activities in Japan. War history is represented in far more detail in local or private museums than in national ones, many events in memory of lost soldiers and air raid victims are organized locally, there is prominent prefectural-level media coverage of regional history (such as in the *Niigata Nippō* newspaper that Gregory Hadley has drawn on extensively in his research), and it is local boards of education that decide which textbooks the children in their jurisdiction use or which (local) museums they can visit on school trips.

Field of Spears is an invaluable contribution to the vast literature of the Pacific War precisely because it engages directly the much-neglected yet important local aspects of war history in Japan. While it recounts in fine yet often uncomfortable detail the experiences of the Jordan Crew on the downed B-29, it is also a fascinating insight into some of the local history activities in Japan that are rarely published in English. *Field of Spears* is also notable for laying bare the problems of reconstructing definitive accounts of the past when the evidence is contradictory and the survivors are often unwilling to speak candidly of their experiences, whether out of a fear of saying what they know or reluctance to drag up such painful memories through the act of testifying.

But the true appeal of Hadley's narrative is in the fallible, human face that it puts on a history of people in extreme life-and-death situations. Within the burgeoning field of war memories and commemoration, discussions of Japanese war memories continue to be predominantly state-centric and focus on diplomatic spats or how the Japanese government responds to ongoing war responsibility issues. This study of local history that utilizes contemporary documents and photographs, media reportage and the author's own interviews with survivors on both sides of the incident provides a refreshing new perspective on war history in Japan through the intriguing story of the events that took place in a quiet corner of Niigata prefecture in late July 1945.

Dr. Philip Seaton
Institute of Language and Culture Studies
Hokkaido University
www.philipseaton.net

PREFACE

History has a way of catching up with people – and in a time and place that they least expect.

For me history happened during a trip to England in the summer of 2002. I was driving through the scenic Cotswold Hills with a colleague who is interested in military history. He asked if I could find out why the Japanese city of Niigata had been removed from the list of potential atomic bomb targets towards the end of the Second World War. I looked at the ancient stone cottages as we passed them by and dimly remembered stories that I had heard soon after moving to Niigata about 'The B-29' – of it burning brightly in the night sky, and of parachutes. I wondered if this incident had anything to do with my colleague's question.

When I returned to Niigata at the end of that summer I discovered that there was no relationship between the 'B-29' and Niigata being removed from the A-bomb target list. However, soon after I had located documents explaining why Niigata was spared the fate of Hiroshima and Nagasaki, my curiosity was sparked about the stories I had heard about the mysterious 'B-29'. Who were the people on that plane? What had happened to them? With over half a century passed, and given the taboo in Japan of talking about those dark days, would it be possible for me, a foreigner, to learn anything?

My search set me on a three year quest that would lead through small Japanese farming villages, dusty archives and rural American towns. Along the way I interviewed scholars, survivors from the B-29 crew, local eyewitnesses, former prisoners of war, and old soldiers. All were initially suspicious and uncertain. Despite the lingering differences and animosity caused by their experiences in the War, the Japanese villagers and B-29 crewmen were united in their common desire to be heard, to be remembered, and to be understood. In telling their stories, each had something valuable to share – and something dreadful to hide.

This book is not what I had first intended to write. The path that I initially took was an analytical approach that would be of interest primarily to war historians and scholars in comparative cultural studies. After three years of detective work, and finding myself surrounded by piles of military reports, unpublished manuscripts by eyewitnesses, war diaries, photos, and documents recently declassified by the US Freedom of Information Act, a realization of the horror and confusion of the incident became clearer. My attempts to express this in an analytical style, however, pushed me further away from the richness of the historical accounts. I decided that the best way to approach this book was in the form of a narrative. My attempt here has been to relate, as authentically as I can, the viewpoints of both the surviving B-29 crewmen and of the villagers who captured them. At the same time, I have sought to place their stories within the wider context of the Pacific Theatre during the closing days of the Second World War.

Many aspects of this story remain steeped in mystery and controversy. While the unsolved elements add to the power of the tale's telling, it has been the controversial parts that have caused me considerable internal struggle. It goes without saying that in war people can make mistakes and do things that they may regret later on. During interviews I felt a growing sense of respect and compassion for the people on both sides of this conflict, and this forced me to face some hard questions: Do I conceal aspects of this story out of consideration for the participants' families and descendants, who often have an interest in preserving for posterity the brave deeds of their forefathers? Or, should I write everything that I have learned, even if it risks a descent into sensationalism? How can I negotiate a balance between professional detachment on the one hand and sentiment on the other? Ultimately, for the sake of showing the effects of war on ordinary people, I decided that all of the story, or at least as much of it as I was able to discover, should be told. At the same time, I feel that this story should be told with compassion. Thus, wherever possible, the use of names has been avoided. It will be up to you, the reader, to decide whether I have succeeded in providing a balanced and considerate account.

A note should be made concerning the Japanese names and script used in the references. In Japan, family names are followed by the given name, although many Japanese living abroad may adopt the western convention of first name followed by family name. For the sake of consistency, throughout this book I have written all names using the western convention. I have also preserved the Japanese text in the footnotes for the primary sources. This has been done so that historians with knowledge of Japanese can follow up the source texts and interviews used to support this book.

This book would not have been possible but for the courage of the Jordan Crew and the residents of Niigata who, though fragile with age, still found it within themselves to recall the trauma of those terrible days. They were often encouraged by their families to talk about this period, which for some had remained a forbidden topic. During the painful and sometimes disturbing process of sharing their experiences some were able to come to terms with their darker memories and embrace them as part of their families' lasting heritage.

A number of Japanese educators, researchers and historians have also been immensely helpful in this research. Much of the research presented in this book has been known for many years by some Japanese scholars, but because it has never been translated into English for a wider audience it has remained somewhat unknown. Researchers provided me with rare documents, photos, memoirs and interviews of villagers that they had conducted during their own investigations. As we shared notes and spoke together, we found ourselves hoping that, by recording this tragic tale, the futile cycles of warfare and violence, themes that are all too frequent in both our countries' histories, might somehow be broken in the lives of others – even for just a moment.

INTRODUCTION

The date is July 19, 1945. A B-29 'Superfortress' bomber, attached to the United States Army Air Forces' 6th Bombardment Group under the command of Captain Gordon Jordan, takes off from the western Pacific island of Tinian on a routine night-time mining mission to Niigata, on the north-western coast of Japan's main island of Honshu. The plane is unexpectedly hit by anti-aircraft fire and goes down in a muddy potato field between the former villages of Yokogōshi and Kyōgase, a few kilometers south-east of Niigata City.

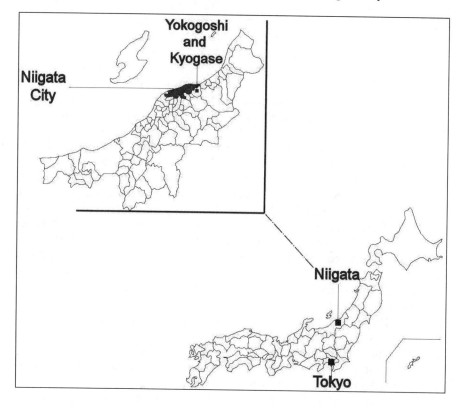

Location of Niigata and the former villages of Yokogōshi and Kyōgase.
Yokogōshi was incorporated into Niigata City and Kyōgase became part of the new Agano City in early 2005.

The cold facts of this incident would probably have remained a footnote on the fading pages of Second World War history were it not for its unique legacy to the city of Niigata. The Jordan Crew's last mission marked a number of firsts. It was the only time that a B-29 was shot down over Niigata City, the first

1

time for anyone to parachute into the prefecture, and it was also the first and only time for women, who were being trained to fight with bamboo spears as part of Japan's final defense against the anticipated Allied invasion, actually to use their primitive weapons against armed American soldiers.[1]

For Japanese who saw the plane go down it has been the iconic B-29, more than the people inside it, which has stood out in their minds. Such is the dehumanizing nature of war, in which weapons of mass destruction often overshadow the memory of the people left in their wake. There remain gaping holes in the local historical records about the men who went down with that B-29 on that night in July 1945. Besides the obvious fact that Japan and America were at war, what were the events that put them over Niigata, and what happened after their plane was shot down? Equally important for the younger generations of the region who know little about 'Niigata's War', and who in my opinion have become increasingly nationalistic in recent years, what are the memories of those who had witnessed the crash and the crew's eventual capture?

This book, however, is not intended only for the people of Niigata. For those living outside of Japan, stories of how soldiers survived the trauma of captivity, torture and starvation have been an enduring American genre since the French and Indian War, and similar literature can be found in other western countries with an imperial history.[2] Numerous books have been written about America's and Japan's historic clash of cultures and of the Allied POW experience in Japan, but these works typically present one side of the conflict. In this book I will look at both Japanese and Allied viewpoints during the incident in Niigata as an example of what happens to ordinary people in obscure places during those inevitable cycles in history when hatred becomes institutionalized. In a very real sense, there are no heroes in this story – only survivors.

Shunji Sato, an eyewitness to the events that transpired on July 20, wrote that local memories about what happened that night are 'hidden in [the] heart, confused and jumbled like the cocoon of a silkworm. But if one can find that strand which makes the cocoon and begins to unravel it, an honest account can be written.'[3] This is a common feature of oral histories and attempts to record traumatic war memories. Some historians argue that narrative inquiries lack rigor. They rightly point out that human beings are imperfect. People forget and memories can be altered, skewed by one's viewpoint or even created from repeated exposure to films, books or the stories of other comrades. Key information can be consciously or unconsciously censored, and some informants will lie, in order to influence the historical record.[4]

Some, if not all, of these problems can also be found in written documents. So the concerns expressed by conservative historians are unwarranted so long as conscientious efforts are made to verify events from other sources.[5] My attempt to document the story of the Jordan Crew and the memories of Niigata citizens has, whenever possible, compared oral interviews with written documents, such as war diaries of the Jordan Crew, military reports, American and Japanese archival materials closer to the time of the incident, and a rare cache of photos which revealed scenes of the crew's capture.

2

Borrowing from Sato's analogy of unraveling the silkworm's cocoon, I will begin by sorting out the confused and jumbled threads of stories told by the survivors of the Jordan Crew. Their missions and the personalities of the crewmen will be examined within the larger tapestry of events that eventually put them over Niigata. The frayed edges of life in Niigata near the end of the war will then be considered. The second part of this book untangles the memories of the Jordan Crew's last mission and those who were living in the villages on the outskirts of Niigata. Based on interviews and historical documents I will weave together a complex fabric of the conflicting accounts of what took place in darkened rice paddies and of the grisly aftermath following the crash. The final part of this book then intertwines the postwar investigations with the efforts that villagers made to cover up the truth of what happened that night over sixty years ago. I will also discuss the lives of the surviving crew and villagers as each sought to deal with the rags of their wartime experiences and move on with their lives.

The Jordan Crew's loss over Niigata was a singular event in the region's history, unsullied by the confusion of multiple downings such as those that took place in other parts of Japan. The incident occurred close enough to a major city to be well-documented from various viewpoints. This book not only provides a good case study of what typically happened to B-29 crewmen shot down over Japan during the Second World War, it is also a forbidding reminder of the *danse macabre* played out in today's wars, when military personnel fall into the waiting arms of frightened, angry civilians.

---

[1] 金塚友之亟 (Tomoyuki Kanazuka), '横越村焼山へ落ちた B29 と京ヶ瀬村へ降りた落下傘 (The B-29 that went down in Yokogōshi and those who parachuted into Kyōgase),' 郷土新潟 (Hometown Niigata) 6 (February 1965), 9.
[2] Robert Doyle, *Voices from Captivity* (Lawrence, Kansas: University of Kansas Press, 1994), 1-6.
[3] 佐藤俊司 (Shunji Sato), '一九四五年七月二十日京ヶ瀬村の一日 (B29 焼山に落つ) (July 20, 1945: A Day in Kyōgase Village [The B-29 Downing in Yakeyama]),' 村誌 (Village Historical Record), 十一月 (November), 平成 14 年 (2002), 148.
[4] Trevor Lummis, 'Structure and Validity in Oral Evidence,' in Robert Perks and Alastair Thomson (eds), *The Oral History Reader*, (London and New York: Routledge, 1998), 273-83.
[5] Ronald J. Grele, 'Movement without Aim: Methodological and Theoretical Problems in Oral History,' in Robert Perks and Alastair Thomson (eds), 38-52.

PART ONE

BACKGROUNDS

CHAPTER ONE

THE JORDAN CREW

In 2002, just as I began my research for this book, five elderly members of the Jordan Crew were still alive and residing in small communities scattered across the United States. Each was initially surprised, then suspicious, when contacted by this unknown researcher from Niigata, the city which reminded them of some of the darkest moments in their lives. One ultimately chose not to talk about the painful memories he had of those days. Four others agreed to share their stories. The son of another member, who was only a toddler when his father died in Niigata, provided a copy of his father's war diary. This is their story.

Captain Gordon Jordan: The Early Years

Captain Gordon Jordan in July 1945.
(Photo courtesy of Robert Grant.)

5

Captain Gordon 'Porky' Jordan (1918-1977) was born on a small farm outside of Monroe, Louisiana. From an early age, he was fascinated by airplanes and wanted to be a pilot. He had very little interest in going on to college, but he went to Louisiana State University for two years so that he could fulfill the minimum educational requirements for becoming an Army Air Force pilot. In early 1941 Gordon was assigned to the 3rd Bomb Squadron and then later to the 397th Heavy Bomb Squadron in the Panama Canal Zone. Even before the United States had entered the Second World War, Jordan had logged hundreds of hours on patrols that scoured the Caribbean for German U-Boats.[1] Because of his experience, in 1943 Jordan was offered the chance to become a test pilot on a secret weapons project. He declined, saying that he was ready for real combat. It was not until later that Jordan learned that the weapons being tested were prototypes for the atomic bomb. Jordan was transferred back to the States, where he began training as a B-29 pilot.[2]

Gordon's Plane: The B-29 Superfortress

The B-29 was one of several planes developed during the early 1940s under the direction of General Henry 'Hap' Arnold. Fearing that war with Germany was imminent and that Great Britain would fall to Hitler's forces, Arnold wanted a Very Long Range (VLR) bomber that could reach European targets from America's eastern coast.[3] The development and production of the bomber cost nearly twice as much as was needed to create the atomic bomb, and the combined costs for building even one B-29 was equivalent to that of a naval cruiser. At Arnold's request, the US Joint Chiefs of Staff put the 'three billion dollar gamble' under his direct command.

Although originally intended for the European theatre, it was clear by 1943 that Germany was losing the war. Arnold unilaterally decided that the B-29s would be used exclusively for the Pacific theatre, ostensibly because only the B-29 had the range to reach Japanese targets from far-flung bases in China and India.[4] The costs of developing the B-29 mounted, and criticism grew that the project was a prime example of pork-barrel politics. But public support was galvanized in favor of the bomber through a series of masterful propaganda films, such as *Target Tokyo* (narrated by a young Ronald Reagan), and *Birth of the B-29*, which linked the plane's development with an American sense of cultural and technological superiority.[5] Exacting revenge upon the Japanese was also a prominent theme.

> The function of the people's Superfortress is to break the race that turned their backs on reason…to spin them around to face a peaceful way of living…it is the people's answer to all the sneak raids, to all the death marches, to all the stabs in the back.[6]

During its heyday, the B-29 was the largest and most advanced bomber ever built, with a wing span of 43 meters, a length of 30 meters, a flight range of over 9000 kilometers, and a service height of 9,700 meters, requiring the first use of pressurized cabins in a bomber. The B-29 bristled with defensive guns and had tracking systems which were guided by a rudimentary analog computer. B-29s could carry over 7000 kilograms of bombs or naval mines. The latest military technology of the time, such as radar and the Norden bombsight, gave crews the potential for hitting targets with greater accuracy than ever before. The bomber was manned by eleven crewmen, who occupied separate fore and aft cabins in the fuselage of the bomber. The cabins were connected by a small pressurized tunnel over the bomb bays.

The Jordan Crew's B-29.
(Photo courtesy of 6th Bomb Group/William Webster.)

Pilots such as Jordan were excited to fly the B-29. Unfortunately, the technology and resources available during the late 1930s and early 1940s meant that developers were hard-pressed to get it off the drawing board, let alone off the ground. In its early days of development, engineers concluded that the B-29 was unsafe and should be discontinued.[7] However, the military knowingly forced the B-29 into production before most of its defects could be corrected.[8] Jordan and his crew were soon to discover that their plane was seriously flawed. Engines sometimes stopped in mid-flight or erupted into flame, bomb bay doors would not close, and unpredictable fuel consumption nearly killed the crew on several occasions.

Memories of Captain Jordan

Jordan frequently repeated the old adage that 'there are old pilots, and bold pilots, but there're no old, bold pilots.' He was extremely careful in the air and expected

7

his crew to follow his example.[9] Jordan is remembered not only for his attention to detail, but also for his skill in flying a plane that was, at the best of times, slow and clumsy. He could often use the jet stream to his advantage when they were low on fuel, and astound his crew by returning to base ahead of other planes.[10] On numerous missions Jordan's plane was severely damaged by anti-aircraft fire, yet he still managed to get his crew back to base alive.

A quality that impressed Jordan's crew was their captain's keen interest in their duty stations and responsibilities. Jordan felt that a B-29 pilot, whose official designation was Air Commander, should be able to perform every major task on a plane in case of an emergency. He asked his crew to teach him how to navigate, operate the radio and radar, read navigation equipment, use the bomb controls, and man the defensive machine gun turrets. He also devoted time to the study of languages. Besides speaking Spanish from his time in Panama, he studied Japanese from a second-generation Japanese American bombardier on Tinian, just in case he was ever shot down. This combination of foresight and attention to detail made a lasting impression on the crew and some emulated Jordan's work ethic when they returned home from the war.[11]

Jordan was older than most of his crew, who were in their early twenties and looked up to him as an elder brother. Mischief is common among young men who band together, but Jordan would not tolerate horseplay or joking during missions. While in the air Jordan was generally taciturn and forbiddingly focused, even during moments of extreme danger. But he could suddenly haul crewmen over the coals if he felt they were not taking things seriously or not performing their duties according to his high standards.[12] Jordan's planes were never decorated with nicknames or the now-famous nose art. This practice was discouraged throughout the 6th Bombardment Group and Jordan saw his B-29s for what they were – tools for doing a dirty job.[13] He and his crew had a serious task ahead and he didn't want them wasting their time on such trivial pursuits.[14]

Jordan worked hard and played hard. Off duty he was laid-back and loved to eat and drink with his crew. Being 185 centimeters tall and weighing in at around 105 kilos earned him the wartime nickname of 'Porky' as a term of endearment. Jordan frequently invited the enlisted crewmen over to the Officers' Club for drinks and would regularly hold small parties with the crew in his Quonset hut. Everyone shared their liquor allotment or care packages from home and treated each other equally regardless of rank. Together they would drink, play cards and get to know each other as they talked and joked through the night.[15]

Jordan took every opportunity to foster this *esprit de corps* among his crewmen. After a mission in early June 1945, his crew's bombing accuracy had been so impressive that Col. Kenneth Gibson, the Commanding Officer of the 6th Bombardment Group, came by Jordan's hut and personally gave the officers a cooler full of beer – quite a treat on hot, tropical Tinian. His thirsty officers wanted to break into the beer right away, but Jordan wouldn't let them touch it until all the crew could be gathered. 'We earned this as a crew, and we'll share it as a crew,' said Jordan.[16]

This is not to say that Jordan was without flaws. Fellow officers and crew also described him as something of a maverick. He loved to gamble and was not adverse to a little wheeling and dealing in order to obtain some of the few creature comforts that could be had on base. Later, as missions dragged on and became increasingly perilous, the crew noticed that Jordan's drinking sometimes got the better of him, though they are quick to say that none of this affected his ability and skill as a pilot.[17] Those closest to Jordan pointed out in an indirect manner that his vices did not go unnoticed by his superiors. Although the Army Air Force had the fastest rate of promotion of any of the branches of the US military during the war, Jordan was still a Captain at a time when other pilots his age had already been promoted to Major or Colonel. Jordan never seemed to show much concern about this. He loved flying, viewed the ladder of military promotion with quiet derision, and focused on taking care of his crew.[18]

Undated photo believed to be that of Jordan (circled) with
friends at the 9th Bombardment Group Officer's Club.
(Richard Keenan. *The 20th Air Force Album*.
Washington, DC: 20th Air Force Association, 1982, 95.)

One crewman was reminded of this during a mission to Rashin, Korea on July 16, 1945. This was the longest bombing mission of the Second World War, and on the return flight, Jordan's plane was dangerously low on fuel. Jordan radioed in a request for an emergency landing at the airfield on American occupied Iwo Jima. When instructed by flight control to maintain a holding pattern until further instructions, Jordan barked back, 'to hell with that,' and proceeded to land the plane.[19] This frequent disregard for procedure put Jordan even further at odds with his superiors, but his willingness to risk disciplinary action to save the lives of his crew, combined with his playful roguishness off duty, only further deepened the sense of fierce loyalty and deep respect that his crew felt for him.

The Jordan Crew

Most of the men of the Jordan Crew had grown up in the small towns and farms that dot rural America. In general, the crew represented a cross section of the United States' white working-class. Some, like Jordan, had joined the Army Air Force before the war. A couple had been drafted, a couple joined out of patriotism, but the majority joined to avoid the strong possibility of being drafted into the Infantry or the Marine Corps. Several on the crew spoke of rumors they heard at the time that being sent to the bloody fronts of the Second World War as a 'ground pounder' was tantamount to a death sentence. A common theme in their interviews was that each had initially wanted to become a pilot, but since the Army Air Force already had a surplus of pilots, they were assigned to less glamorous positions.

The Copilot

First Lieutenant Wails 'Hawk' Hawkins came from Bessemer, Alabama. He spoke with a slow Southern drawl that amused the men on the crew who came from cities outside of the rural South. He came across as socially awkward when paired next to Jordan. Known by his crew as a quiet, hen-pecked, family man who was genuinely kind and a little shy, Hawkins had all the qualities that would make him a good neighbor during peacetime. These strengths, however, became liabilities during combat. On a number of harrowing missions, Hawkins would freeze and could not help Jordan fly the plane. Jordan privately worried about him, as did the other officers.

The Bombardier and Navigator

First Lieutenant Clinton Wride was raised in a Mormon family from Portland, Oregon. He was extremely good-humored and laid-back. He was the only officer who was single. Although Wride was required to study navigation in case of an emergency, he often refused, saying that navigating was for 'peasants'. Instead, he focused on being an excellent bombardier. His station in the nose of the B-29 put him at the forefront of any attacks that the crew experienced in later missions. As time dragged on, his good humor began to fade.

The crew's navigator, First Lieutenant Milton Garin, came from a well-off Jewish family in New York City. He was the only member of the original crew to have completed university.[20] Outgoing, articulate and professional, he enjoyed getting to know everyone on the crew and was Captain Jordan's confidant. The crew relied on him as their good luck charm, since he appeared utterly convinced that anyone who stayed with him would survive the war and return home alive.

The Jordan Crew on Tinian.
Front Row from Left to Right: Capt. Gordon Jordan (Air Commander/Pilot), 1st Lt. Wails Hawkins (Copilot), 1st Lt. Milton Garin (Navigator), 1st Lt. Clinton Wride (Bombardier). Back Row from Left to Right: Staff Sgt. Florio Spero (Tail Gunner), Master Sgt. George McGraw (Flight Engineer), Staff Sgt. Norman Kruvant (Central Fire Control), Sgt. Robert Grant (Left Gunner), Staff Sgt. Max Adams (Radar Operator), Staff Sgt. Robert Burkle (Right Gunner), and Staff Sgt. Walter Wiernik (Radio Operator).
(Photo courtesy of Milton Garin.)

The Flight Engineer and Radio Operator

In addition to his duties as engineer, Master Sergeant George 'Mac' McGraw was also in charge of the enlisted crewmen. McGraw was the next natural leader within the group and had much in common with Jordan. From a farm near the small town of Gillett, Arkansas, he had also been in the Army Air Force before the war. Like Jordan, he was popular with the crew, sociable off duty, and competent during missions. McGraw was serious and made sure that the younger crewmen stayed on-task. He kept a vigilant eye over the fuel consumption gauges and on long missions, when he and other crewmen were allowed to sleep, McGraw would sleep facing these gauges so that they would be the first thing he would see when he opened his eyes.[21] The radio operator was Staff Sergeant Walter Wiernik from Buffalo, New York. A quiet and withdrawn man, he typically kept to himself. Wiernik was, however, respected for being an excellent radio operator, and he could be depended upon to respond quickly during times of crisis.

The Radar Operator

In the aft cabin, a soft-spoken, serious Alabaman, Staff Sergeant Max Adams, acted as the crew's radar operator. He had been a regular Army sergeant for a few years before being transferred to the Army Air Force. Adams was admired for his discipline and self-control, but if put under prolonged stress, he could lose his temper. Adams had a young wife and children waiting for him back at home.

The Gunners

Staff Sergeant Norman Kruvant, from New York, was a band leader before the war and a distant in-law of Milton Garin. A father of two and drafted at the age of 35, he became the central fire controller for the plane. Kruvant could be described as having an artist's temperament. He was a perfectionist and had great difficulty dealing with the anxiety of not being in control of the many unexpected variables during combat missions. The worries he had about what might happen began to grow, and eventually he became disturbingly nervous and emotionally brittle. Garin and Jordan both had concerns about Kruvant during later missions.

Staff Sergeant Robert Burkle hailed from Wheeling, West Virginia. He was the crew's right gunner. Easy-going, and a devout but superstitious Catholic who believed in signs and portents, he got along with everyone in the crew.

Sgt. Robert Grant, from Jamesville, Wisconsin, was the youngest member of the crew. Bright, cheerful and full of life, he was a source of joy for everyone, who simply called him 'the Kid'. Grant served as the left gunner.

At the remote tail-end of the plane was tail gunner Florio Spero. An Italian American from Chicago and with a wife and two young children, Spero had also been drafted. Probably the most misunderstood member of the crew, Spero, or 'Funny' as his friends knew him, was remembered as being mischievous, and frequently had to be bailed out of some sort of problem on base. Sometimes his antics delayed the crew's timetable and this put him further out of Jordan's favor.[22] However, his fellow gunners also remembered that Spero performed well in combat and was the type of person who would give the shirt off of his back to help someone in need.[23] A study of Spero's war diary shows that he had a sensitive, thoughtful side that Jordan and the other officers never saw. Spero and Burkle would sometimes attend Mass together.

The memories of the surviving members of the Jordan Crew about each other reflect a certain frankness that one often finds among a family that has survived a deep trauma, but grown to love one another as a result of their shared experiences. Despite their gruff demeanor and stark honesty during interviews, when they returned to thinking about their fellow crewmen they would speak with compassion and sorrow.

War tends to strip people down to their component strengths and weaknesses, exposed for all to see. Interpersonal conflicts within the crew did exist – something that is to be expected when circumstances suddenly force eleven strangers to live and work together. However, while such dynamics have the potential for tearing a squad apart, Milton Garin explained that the Jordan Crew very quickly became an exceptionally tight- knit group.

> We were all in the same boat, so everybody had a warm feeling towards each other. It was survival. This is our team. We cared for each other. Despite weaknesses I saw in others I had a strong feeling for everyone on the crew, and the others felt the same.[24]

As time went by, the crew's lives became increasingly intertwined. Everyone knew whose marriage was on the rocks, who could be counted on in an emergency, and who needed to be kept out of trouble on base. Without speaking, everyone knew who was scared and who was strong. They had, in effect, become a family.

Early Training and Rites of Passage

The crew assembled at Grand Island, Nebraska in mid-1944 and was assigned to the 24th Squadron of the 6th Bombardment Group, which was attached to the 313th Wing of the 20th Army Air Force. Their early training took place in B-17 'Flying Fortresses', where they flew mock bombing missions over some of the larger metropolitan areas of the Midwest. Later, they prepared for long air missions by making flights from America's heartland to Cuba or Panama.

Like any band of young men in wartime, the Jordan Crew had their share of wild times. Even to this day not all on the crew are comfortable with outsiders knowing everything about their tour of duty, partly because old age has done little to erase feelings of embarrassment over youthful indiscretions, and partly because of the belief that, as a family, there are things that outsiders should never know. What the crew did when they weren't fighting to stay alive was nobody's business but their own. Others on the crew that I spoke with were less protective, feeling instead that a 'matter of fact' account of their days was the best approach. Knowing something of who they were when not in combat only serves to paint a richer picture of the crew as normal men whose lives had been turned on end by war. There is merit to be found in both of these views.

On their down time in Cuba, the crew began to bond together as friends and Jordan introduced them to several of the more colorful establishments near Batista Field. After they finished their advanced training in late December they flew their new B-29 along the route established a few months earlier when the 6th Bombardment Group had made their way to Tinian. They stayed a few days on the airbase at Kearny, Nebraska, to make final preparations.

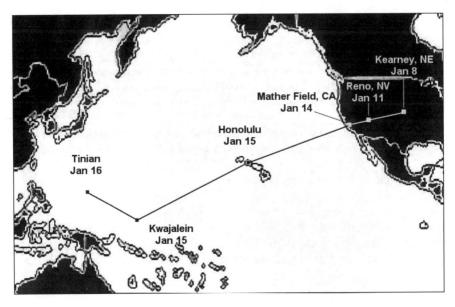

Flight route of the Jordan Crew to Tinian.

Near the base were places that provided companionship and comforts of the sort that some soldiers have sought on the night before going off to war. Some of the crew took advantage of these services before their flight to Reno, Nevada, but soon found to their chagrin that they were in need of other services, this time of a medical nature. When Jordan learned of what had happened he was livid, and gave the men another type of dressing down.[25] Because most of the crewmen came from conservative backgrounds, Jordan's scolding only heightened the sense of embarrassment they felt for what had happened. Several ran out to find the base chaplain for prayers and confession.[26] A quiet and sheepish crew took off for Mather Field a couple of days later. There they rested briefly before flying to Honolulu. They only had a few hours on the island, but some of the crewmen still found time to sneak off and visit Waikiki. Since it was early in the morning, there was little to do or see. After refueling, they flew on to Kwajalein, and finally arrived at Tinian on January 16, 1945.

---

[1] Milton Garin, e-mail message to author, June 30, 2003.

[2] Milton Garin, interview by author, March 20, 2004, MD Recording.

[3] Fiske Hanley, *History of 504th Bombardment Group* (Enfield, Connecticut: 504th Bomb Group Association), 9.

[4] W.F. Craven and J.L. Cate, *The Army Air Forces in World War II* (Chicago: University of Chicago Press, 1953), 12.

[5] *Target Tokyo*, Film, nar. Ronald Reagan, 21:54. (First Motion Picture Unit: Army Air Forces, 1945).

[6] *Birth of the B-29*, Film, US War Department, 20 min. (Army Pictorial Services, Army Air Forces, 1945).

[7] Haywood S. Hansell, *The Air Plan that Defeated Hitler* (Atlanta, GA: Longino & Porter, 1972), 203. Roger Mudd, ann., *Unsung Heroes of the B-29s*, Videocassette, 50 min. (History Channel A&E Network, 2001).

[8] Herman Wolk, 'The Twentieth Against Japan,' *Air Force Magazine*, April, 2004, 68. Roger Mudd, ann., *Unsung Heroes of the B-29s*, Videocassette, 50 min. (History Channel A&E Network, 2001).

[9] William Conine, interview by author, November 29, 2005, notes. Conine is the family historian for the family of George McGraw, and provided additional anecdotes and other material that he had learned from McGraw before his death in March, 2004.

[10] Paul Trump, e-mail message to author, June 29, 2003. George McGraw, interview by author, August 17, 2003, notes.

[11] Milton Garin, March 20, 2004. Paul Trump, interview by author, September 13, 2004, MD Recording. Milton Garin, e-mail message to author, May 13, 2003.

[12] Paul Trump, interview by author, March 23, 2004, MD Recording. Robert Grant, interview by author, April 23, 2004, MD Recording.

[13] W.M. Rice, ed., *Pirate's Log: A Historical Record of the Sixth Bombardment Group* (Manila: 2771st Engr. Base Reproduction Co, 1946), 70.

[14] George McGraw, August 17, 2003.

[15] Paul Trump, March 23, 2004.

[16] Florio Spero, June 10-11, 1945, war diary, Spero Family Collection, Homer Glen, Illinois. Milton Garin, e-mail message to author, May 14, 2003. Milton Garin, e-mail message to author, June 20, 2003.

[17] Sam Parks, interview by author, March 20, 2004, MD Recording. Milton Garin, March 20, 2004. Paul Trump, interview by author, May 14, 2003, notes.

[18] Milton Garin, March 20, 2004.

[19] Paul Trump, March 23, 2004. Florio Spero, July 16, 1945.

[20] Garin is referred to as Milton Garfinkle in war records and documents. He changed his family name to Garin after the war, and at his request, will be referred to as Milton Garin throughout this book.

[21] William Conine, November 29, 2005.

[22] Milton Garin, e-mail message to author, June 23, 2003.

[23] Robert Grant, interview by author, October 29, 2003, CD Recording. Robert Grant, April 23, 2004.

[24] Milton Garin, March 20, 2004.

[25] Milton Garin, June 23, 2003.

[26] Florio Spero, January 9-10, 1945.

CHAPTER TWO

ON THE GROUND AT TINIAN

Tinian is one of several small islands located in what is now the western Pacific archipelago of the Northern Mariana Islands. With a land area of 101 km² it is about twice the size of New York's Manhattan Island, and is the second largest island in the group after Saipan. It was a Spanish colony from the 16th century until 1899, whereupon it was sold to Germany. From 1914 it was a Japanese territory when, as an ally of the US and Britain in the First World War, Japan had won a decisive battle against the German forces stationed there. Imperial Japan then violated treaty agreements and turned Tinian into a military fortress.

Tinian in 1945.
(Photo courtesy of George McGraw.)

The battle for the Mariana Islands, known as Operation Forager, began on June 15, 1944. In the face of determined and well-entrenched Japanese resistance US Marines fought for over two months to secure all of the islands.

American casualties were expected to be especially high in the taking of Tinian. However, intelligence reports suggested that the inter-service rivalries between three Japanese commanders on the island might lead to a disorganized defense. A clever diversion was designed to draw Japanese forces into defending the main town while US Marines invaded from another beach. Lack of coordination among the Japanese forces led to confusion and frustration on the battlefield. Near the end, American field officers reported that many Japanese troops ended their lives in suicidal *banzai* charges or, when wounded, lay among the dead waiting to detonate land mines strapped to their chests.[1] In a tragedy that was to be repeated on Saipan and Okinawa, hundreds of Japanese civilians living on the island jumped to their deaths from cliffs, sometimes at gunpoint from Japanese troops, rather than surrender to American forces.[2]

US Marines Landing on the Northern Beaches
of Tinian, and Japanese Military Casualties.
(Carl Hoffman, *The Seizure of Tinian*, Washington, D.C.: Historical Branch,
G-3 Division, Headquarters, U.S. Marine Corps, 1951, 50, 66.)

Most of the resistance was subdued within a week, and Tinian was virtually under US control by the beginning of July 1944. Because the island was close enough to allow B-29s to strike at the heart of the Japanese Empire, plans had been underway even before the island was secured to convert it into an airfield. The specialist construction battalions of the US Navy, the Seabees, soon began the mammoth task of transforming Tinian from a hard scrabble coral island into what would eventually become the largest military airbase of the Second World War.

The ground crews of the 6th Bomb Group were the first to be shipped to Tinian. These men stayed in two-man 'pup' tents while the Seabees prepared the airstrips and built other basic facilities. Burying the dead was not a priority and piles of Japanese corpses were left to rot only a few hundred feet from their tents. The flies were so numerous that soldiers couldn't eat without swallowing at least one.[3]

Ground crews waiting in pup tents while Navy Seabees
construct the airbase on Tinian in 1944.
(Photo courtesy of 6th Bomb Group/William Webster.)

The few Japanese civilians who had survived the invasion were interned in a squalid village located in the middle of the island. At times they were brought out for work details or to perform on stage for the American troops. Japanese and Korean military POWs were kept in a separate camp. Approximately five-hundred Japanese soldiers refused to surrender and were holed up on the southern end of the island. American commanders considered them a spent force and, instead of risking more casualties, a perimeter was set up using surplus World War One machine guns. Weapons fire was often exchanged, especially during the early days of the American occupation. At night Japanese remnants would sometimes sneak into the airbase on foraging missions or to commit acts of sabotage.

It quickly dawned on the Jordan Crew, or 'Porky's Pigs' as they now called themselves, that they were living in a war zone. Upon arrival each member was issued a side arm and the enlisted men were posted on guard duty. A few days after they had arrived, on January 23, some watched the infantry burn a cane field next to the base. Several Japanese soldiers who had been hiding in the undergrowth emerged from the other side in flight, but all were cut down by a detachment of American troops who had been waiting for them. In retaliation, Japanese soldiers struck back the following day by blowing up an ammunition dump. Twelve US soldiers were killed.[4]

Japanese civilian internment camp (left) and the bombed out ruins of Tinian
Town (right). There was little for soldiers to do off base.
(Richard Keenan. *The 20th Air Force Album*. Washington, DC: 20th Air Force
Association, 1982, 78.)

Early Days

The crew's first bombing mission to the small island of Maug, north of Tinian,
did not count towards the thirty-five needed to rotate back to the US. It was a
short flight that was little more than a training mission, with no flak or fighters.
One of the gunners on the Jordan Crew shot the radar dome of an enemy
listening post. During their first official mission on February 8, over nearby Truk
Island, they encountered only a few distant puffs of flak and minimal fighter
resistance. These early reminders of war were soon forgotten, since the weather
and constant mechanical problems with their B-29 kept the Jordan Crew firmly
on the ground.[5]

As weapons fire from the south became less frequent and the remaining
bodies of war dead found near the edge of the rapidly-developing airbase were
disposed of, Tinian began to feel less like a military base and more like the
Jordan Crew's memories of summer camp when they had been teenage boys.
Perhaps the best summary of life on Tinian for the Jordan Crew can be found in
the lyrics of a song entitled 'Rum and Coca Cola', written by a jazz band formed
from B-29 crewmen stationed on the island:

> Have you ever been to Tinian?
> It's heaven for the enlisted man.
> There's whiskey, girls and such,
> But all are labeled: 'Mustn't touch.'
>
> This tropic isle's a paradise
> Of muddy roads and rainy skies,
> Outdoor latrines and fungus feet,
> And every day more goat to eat.

Enlisted men are on the beam,
Officers say 'we're one big team.'
But do they share their rum and coke?
Ha, ha, ha, that's one big joke![6]

6th Bomb Group Living Area on Tinian in February 1945.
(Photo courtesy of Harry George.)

In the beginning the air crews lived in eight-man pyramidal tents. Insects of all kinds made their visits and crewmen were given a daily supply of DDT to spray on themselves and the vermin. After the daily battle with the bugs, the crew would soon become bored, and at times this led to carelessness. One day Wiernik was cleaning his .45 pistol, unaware that it was still loaded. It discharged and the bullet narrowly missed McGraw's head, passing over his shoulder and leaving a hole in the tent. McGraw had more than a few choice words to share with his junior crewman, once he got over the shock.[7]

With the construction of the base hospital came nurses. While in the beginning most looked quite plain to the crew, they became more attractive with each passing week. Fraternizing with the nurses was strictly forbidden for the enlisted men, but this rule did little to deter some on the Jordan Crew, married or otherwise. Like boys sneaking over to the girls' cabins, they would find increasingly creative ways in which to make their night-time rendezvous. Jordan

20

found himself having to keep his eye on some of his more rambunctious crew members.

The Seabees soon brought running water, showers, refrigeration units and other comforts to the island. All of these were welcome additions, since the hot, tropical weather was only broken by sudden and severe storms that lashed their tents and turned the dry red soil both inside and outside into a thick mire. The base became even more livable after the Seabees finished building Quonset huts to house the air crews. For an extra fee, (usually two or three bottles of bourbon), the Seabees would build a frame out of plywood 'liberated' from the supply house and put over this a rubber mesh out of an inner tube. The result was a bed that was far more comfortable than any standard Army cot. 'Seabee beds', as they were called, were in great demand on Tinian.

Air crew quarters (left) and officers' quarters
sporting one of the much-coveted Seabee beds.
(Richard Keenan. *The 20th Air Force Album*. Washington, DC: 20th Air Force
Association, 1982, 93.)

It took Jordan longer than most to procure one of these beds, as one old friend remembers. It was a typical night over at Jordan's Quonset hut, where a good time was being had with modest stakes at the poker table:

> One of them broke out a bottle and they started drinkin'. And all the sudden Porky started cryin' like you never heard a man cry before. And everybody kept asking him, [they] said, 'What's the matter Porky, what's the matter?' He says, 'Y'all just drank up my Seabee bed!' From then on, we kidded him about someone's drinkin' up his Seabee bed.[8]

Some of the 6th Bomb Group crews began to decorate their huts with latticed sun decks or by planting seeds brought from home. The Jordan Crew's hut was austere in comparison to these attempts to tame the island and erase the reminders of death still lingering over the burned out ruins of Tinian Town. A few pictures of wives hung on the walls. When not at the Officers' Club, Jordan could often be seen on his cot poring over technical manuals for the B-29.[9] Other men on the crew lay around, swam in the ocean, fished, or walked along the rocky beach. Sometimes they scavenged for semi-precious stones or risked popping into the jungle in search of Japanese war trophies. Some days officers listened to Tokyo Rose on the radio or made friends at the newly-erected bar. Enlisted men scrounged around for a beer to supplement their meager allotment and thought up new ways to adjust to the food, which was so poor that they would sneak into their B-29 to eat the emergency rations.[10] These lazy, almost idyllic days were to end shortly with the arrival of their new commanding officer.

Shakeup at the Top

The crew had arrived at Tinian just as the Commander of the 20th Air Force in the Marianas, Brigadier General Haywood Hansell, was to be relieved of command. Hansell had been struggling to turn the B-29 into an effective fighting machine. While he is credited with overcoming immense administrative and logistical problems, his most 'implacable and inscrutable enemy,' as he put it, was the weather.[11] The B-29 was designed to fly at high altitudes, and Hansell was keen on using this technological advantage on daylight precision bombing raids. However, unpredictable tropical weather patterns, the newly-discovered jet stream, and frequent low cloud cover over Japan caused the failure or cancellation of numerous missions.

Generals Haywood Hansell (left) and Curtis LeMay in late January 1945. (Richard Keenan. *The 20th Air Force Album*. Washington, DC: 20th Air Force Association, 1982, 61.)

At one time during his tenure, in only seven missions, over 180 men were lost. Sixty percent of these losses resulted from B-29s going down in the ocean on the return because they had either run out of fuel or had experienced unknown mechanical failures. Hansell's high altitude precision tactics were not working. Only one bomb in fifty had landed within 1000 feet of the target point.[12]

Hansell's commander, General 'Hap' Arnold, was starting to lose face with his peers on the Joint Chiefs of Staff. Arnold believed that the B-29 alone would be able to force a Japanese surrender and mitigate the need for a costly land invasion. But so far his B-29s had failed either to dent Japanese war production or affect Japanese morale. The timetable for an invasion of the Japanese home islands had been set for November 1945 and Arnold needed to deliver dramatic results if he was going to vindicate himself and set the stage for an Independent Air Force. He replaced Hansell with Major General Curtis LeMay in late January 1945.

June 22, 1945 photo of one of the three different B-29s flown by the Jordan Crew.
On early missions their plane itself was a greater threat than enemy fire.
(Photo courtesy of Robert Grant.)

In the beginning, LeMay's transfer to the 20th did little to solve the problems that were cropping up everywhere. On February 12 the Jordan Crew witnessed one B-29 explode on take off, instantly killing the entire crew. Another B-29 crew in the 6th Bombardment Group was lost on the same day forty-five minutes after take off when one engine failed and another burst into flames.[13] On February 15 the Jordan Crew had their own close call when a prop governor broke on one of their engines just seconds before take off. On February 25 the crew was two hours away from a high altitude precision mission over Tokyo when they suddenly discovered they could not access the fuel in their bomb bay tanks. They barely made it back. They had further problems during the next mission on March 4 when, after they had dropped their bombs on a high altitude mission over Tokyo, one of their engines experienced serious problems. Jordan shut down the engine (a process called feathering) before it could catch fire and the crew made it back to Tinian.[14] Because of the overcast conditions and confusion among flight leaders, the mission was unsuccessful.[15]

A Change in Strategy

These first few weeks of continuing with Hansell's high altitude daylight precision bombing tactics had put LeMay's military career in jeopardy. Arnold's Committee on Operational Analysis (COA) began to insist on incendiary attacks similar to those used on Germany. The COA had plans on the drawing board since 1943 that called for incendiary attacks on civilian targets. Fire-bombing would wipe out the cottage industries dispersed throughout the major cities that COA believed were serving as an important link in the chain of Japan's war production. While some historians have claimed that incendiary attacks were also intended to demoralize the Japanese populace, Thomas Searle makes the convincing case that strategists fully intended to kill the thousands of civilians who worked in Tokyo's factories. His conclusion is based upon a study of USAAF documents that indicate large numbers of Japanese civilian casualties as a primary objective.[16]

Some in Washington DC, such as Secretary of War Henry Stimson, were concerned that incendiary attacks would give the US a reputation of 'outdoing Hitler in atrocities.'[17] Hansell seems to have been in this camp. He had earlier been ordered by Arnold to attempt incendiary attacks, but most of his efforts were unsuccessful since they were conducted from high altitudes.[18] Hansell wrote years later in his memoirs that such tactics were not only inaccurate and wasteful, they were also a violation of America's air doctrine.[19]

However, the fact that Tokyo was a tinderbox had been in the minds of American generals even before the war. George C. Marshall stated a month before the Japanese attack on Pearl Harbor that 'if war with the Japanese does come, we'll fight mercilessly. Flying Fortresses will be dispatched immediately to set the paper cities of Japan on fire. There won't be any hesitation about bombing civilians – it will be all-out.'[20] Most in Washington DC held similar views. Deputy Secretary of Defense Robert Lovett stated that 'if we are going to have a total war, we might as well make it as horrible as possible.'[21]

In such a climate, General Curtis LeMay was the ideal soldier for what was to come. Hard, crass, gruff, and chomping his trademark cigar butt, LeMay had gained a reputation for being utterly ruthless. He showed little or no remorse for inflicting devastating numbers of casualties upon the enemy or when risking staggering losses among his men, if he felt that doing so would achieve military objectives:

...if you are going to use military force, then you ought to use overwhelming military force. Use too much and deliberately use too much...You'll save lives, not only your own, but the enemy's too.[22]

Against the reservations of most of his staff, LeMay decided on the controversial and unconventional strategy of low altitude night-time incendiary attacks. He based his decision partly from what he had learned from his operations officer, Robert McNamara, (who would go on to become the Secretary of Defense during the Kennedy and Johnson Administrations), that Japanese anti aircraft batteries were calibrated for extremely high altitudes in an attempt to get at the B-29s. LeMay gambled that Japanese anti-aircraft crews would be unable to adjust quickly enough to low altitude attacks.[23] He was right.

The March Blitz Begins

In early March of 1945 LeMay ordered the protective armor stripped out of the B-29s and for the heavier canons used for point defense to be removed. He then directed the planes to be loaded with additional incendiary cluster bombs and for them to attack Tokyo at an altitude of 1,500 meters. The Jordan Crew were among many who were concerned about the nature of flying their lumbering B-29s at such low altitudes, to which LeMay is reported to have replied, 'Then I won't have too many planes in my command. We have to hit the Japanese targets, and I can always get replacement aircraft and crews.'[24]

The resultant raid on Tokyo was, for its time, the most destructive air attack in history. Estimates vary, but historians generally agree that approximately 100,000 citizens died in one night.[25] The Jordan Crew's impressions of this mission depended largely upon their educational background and the degree to which they had personalized the attack on Pearl Harbor or internalized the reports of atrocities committed by the Japanese army during the Bataan Death March. For those on the crew with less education and life experience, such as Spero, the March 9 mission was described as '...boy, that's the most beautiful fire I ever seen...all of Tokyo was burning.'[26] Garin, whose schooling had allowed him to become classmates with the daughter of a Japanese diplomat who had been recalled to Tokyo just before the war, looked at the same inferno below, steeled his resolve, and hoped that his friend was still alive.[27]

Very few B-29s were lost on this mission and LeMay, or 'Old Ironass' as his men called him (out of earshot), was hailed as a hero. The Japanese media, however, gave him another name that day: 'Brutal LeMay'.[28] McNamara recalls the time he spent with LeMay after the attack on Tokyo.

I think the issue is not so much incendiary bombs. I think the issue is: in order to win a war should you kill 100,000 people in one night, by firebombing or any other way? LeMay's answer would be clearly 'Yes.' Was there a rule then that said you shouldn't bomb, shouldn't kill, shouldn't burn to death 100,000 civilians in one night? LeMay said, 'If we'd lost the war, we'd all have been prosecuted as war criminals.' And I think he's right. He, and I'd say I, were behaving as war criminals. LeMay recognized that what he was doing would be thought immoral if his side had lost. But what makes it immoral if you lose and not immoral if you win?[29]

LeMay could have quoted the old Japanese saying of *kateba kangun,* or 'the victorious army is vindicated.' LeMay was not alone in his belief that the firebombing of Tokyo was justified. General Ira Eaker, Arnold's deputy, stated that 'it made a lot of sense to kill skilled workers by burning whole areas.'[30] It was only after the war that most Americans sought to distance themselves from their support of LeMay and others to fire-bomb Japan.

Typical anti-Japanese propaganda poster during the war.
(NARA.)

During the war the American public was largely ambivalent about the Japanese civilian casualties resulting from the air campaign.[31] This was due in no small part to the publicity given to the appalling behavior of the conquering Japanese armies and the racist propaganda that relentlessly portrayed the Japanese as vicious and sub-human. Along with LeMay, most believed that fire-bombing was the quickest way to neutralize Japan's military capabilities and end the war.[32]

In the 'March Blitz' LeMay used every fire-bomb in his arsenal on Japan's major urban centers. Jordan's crew participated in a number of these missions, which decimated Japanese war industries and resulted in more civilian deaths than the combined atomic bombings of Hiroshima and Nagasaki.

The Jordan Crew nearly became mingled themselves with the ashes rising from the massive funeral pyres below during their March 19 mission over Nagoya. After dropping their bombs, they were caught in a thermal draft that blasted their B-29 upward into a 'slow roll', much in the way a dry autumn leaf is blown aloft in a bonfire. After a struggle Gordon was finally able to get their plane back under control. They diverted to Iwo Jima for an emergency landing.[33] Although they discovered that several bolts were missing, to their amazement, the plane seemed to be intact. McGraw noted, however, that it handled more sluggishly after this incident.[34] They returned to Tinian the day after to join the festivities being held on base celebrating the success of the campaign, and to receive medals for flying on four of the seven incendiary raids.

Jordan Crew Navigator Milton Garin (center) receiving an air medal from Col. Kenneth Gibson for his part in the Tokyo Firebombings.
(Photo courtesy of the 6th Bomb Group.)

Results of the Blitz

Although it was discovered after the war that most of the cottage industries had already been closed down by the beginning of the war and that manufacturing had been centralized in the larger factories,[35] the Blitz was successful in its main objectives of crippling Japanese war production and killing large numbers of skilled workers. However, it did little to demoralize the Japanese citizenry. If anything, as in Germany a few months earlier, and in Britain in 1940, the tactic had the opposite effect.[36] Across Japan, hatred burned against the Americans flying the B-29s. Japanese propagandists claimed the moral high ground while concealing the fact that their own military had already caused some 300,000 deaths in China from their campaign of aerial bombardment, which included chemical and biological weapons.[37] Even if the Japanese public had known more about the atrocities in China it is doubtful whether any change in wartime attitudes would have taken place. Chinese casualties were not Japanese casualties.

In retaliation there were numerous incidents in Southern Japan of POWs being executed and the treatment of captured B-29 crews changed markedly. American military archives are replete with reports of civilians wielding a vicious assortment of kitchen and farming implements and killing crewmen who bailed out over Japan. Ironically, and in contrast to the earlier response in Germany, nearly all of the crewmen who lived to tell their stories were rescued by the Japanese military. The Imperial Army believed that B-29 crewmen knew vital information about the anticipated invasion of the home islands.[38] Airmen were placed in special custody and the Jordan Crew would soon learn about the type of treatment that awaited these unfortunate prisoners.

Operation Starvation

The Navy now insisted on having its turn with the B-29. Codenamed Operation Starvation, major shipping lanes were to be mined in order to cut off the supply of raw materials from Japan's north-eastern colonies and thereby reduce the Empire's capacity to wage war. LeMay put the 313th Wing on Tinian in charge of the entire operation. Beginning in late March 1945 low altitude night-time missions started in the Shimonoseki Straits that separate Honshū from the south-western island of Kyūshū. Mine warfare had not been a standard American tactic in earlier conflicts, so this change caught the Japanese high command by surprise. The Japanese navy had an especially difficult task sweeping for the various mines (magnetic, acoustic and pressure-sensitive) deployed by B-29s.

The loss of the Shimonoseki Straits was devastating for Japan. In all over 13,000 mines were dropped, resulting in the sinking or disabling of over a thousand ships.[39] Transport became virtually impossible in all of Japan's southern ports. Shipping and military supply lines were all but cut in other major ports.[40] In contrast to the fire-bombings, the physical and psychological effects of Operation Starvation on the Japanese people were far-reaching and further contributed to a decline in wartime production as well as to a virtual meltdown of the Japanese economy.[41] Captain Kyugo Tamura, Chief of the Mine Section of the Naval Technical Department in Tokyo, was interrogated after the war and gave this frank assessment.

> The result of B-29 mining was so effective against the shipping that it eventually starved the country. I think you probably could have shortened the war by beginning earlier.[42]

28

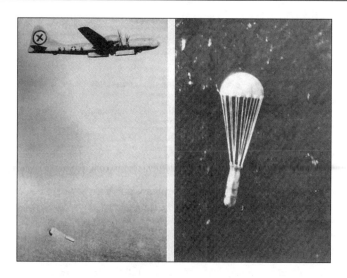

9th Bombardment Group B-29 on an aerial mining mission. Mines were torpedo-shaped and dropped from parachutes to avoid detonation upon impact. (Richard Keenan. *The 20th Air Force Album*. Washington, DC: 20th Air Force Association, 1982, 97.)

With the major shipping ports choked with mines, Japan shifted its supply lines to its secondary and tertiary ports. Of these, Niigata, codenamed later by the US as 'Minefield UNCLE', rapidly became Japan's lifeline to desperately-needed raw materials.[43]

The Jordan Crew did not participate in these early mining missions. However, the skill and efficiency of Jordan and his crew had been noticed and they were sent to Lead Crew School. Lead crews were reserved for the most dangerous missions and night-time mining missions were considered 'milk runs' to be given to the less experienced crews.[44] After a few weeks of Lead Crew training, they were back on daylight precision bombing missions over Kanoya Airfield, Nagoya, Okinawa and Tokyo.

Their plane, however, had become increasingly dangerous to fly. An engine blew a piston halfway to the target on April 12 and on April 28, with no fighters or flak over Kanoya Airfield, their plane lost two engines just after they had bombed their target. They again barely made it back to Tinian. Soon afterwards, they 'traded' their old B-29 with a hapless crew just arriving with one of the latest models.[45]

---

[1] Carl Hoffman, *The Seizure of Tinian* (Washington, DC: Historical Branch, G-3 Division, Headquarters, U.S. Marine Corps, 1951), 41-65, 124, http://www.ibiblio.org/hyperwar/USMC/USMC-M-Tinian/index.html. (accessed May 24, 2005).

[2] W.M. Rice, ed., *Pirate's Log: A Historical Record of the Sixth Bombardment Group* (Manila: 2771st Engr. Base Reproduction Co, 1946), 26.

[3] Virgil Morgan, e-mail message to author, June 7, 2006.

[4] Florio Spero, January 23-30, 1945, war diary, Spero Family Collection, Homer Glen, Illinois. W.M. Rice, ed., *Pirate's Log*, 29.

[5] Florio Spero, February 8, 1945.

[6] Tony Adrean (Cpl), 'Have you ever been to Tinian?,' *Brief*, August 14, 1945, 14.

[7] Florio Spero, March 8, 1945.

[8] Sam Parks, interview by author, March 20, 2004, MD Recording.

[9] Milton Garin, e-mail message to author, June 22, 2006.

[10] Robert Grant, interview by author, April 23, 2004, MD Recording.

[11] Haywood S. Hansell, *The Strategic Air War Against Germany & Japan: A Memoir* (Washington, DC: Office of Air Force History, United States Air Force, 1986), 203.

[12] Christopher Lew, 'Trial by fire: The strategic bombing of Japan,' *World War II Magazine*, September, 1995, http://history1900s.about.com/library/prm/bltrialbyfire1.htm. (accessed May 10, 2005).

[13] W.M. Rice, 29. Florio Spero, February 12, 1945.

[14] Florio Spero, March 4, 1945.

[15] W.M. Rice, 32.

[16] Thomas R. Searle, 'It made a lot of sense to kill skilled workers: The Firebombing of Tokyo in March 1945,' *Journal of Military History*, 66, no. 1 (2002), 133.

[17] Henry Stimson, Washington DC, June 6, 1945, diary, Henry Lewis Stimson Papers, Manuscripts and Archives, Yale University, New Haven, Connecticut, http://www.doug-long.com/stimson5.htm. (accessed December 17, 2005).

[18] Christopher Lew. The only exception took place during the final mission under Hansell's command, in which B-29s were ordered to approach at slightly lower altitudes over the city of Akashi, due to heavy cloud cover. This mission was the most successful during Hansell's tenure, but LeMay was already on his way to Tinian with orders to relieve him of command.

[19] Haywood S. Hansell, 11, 169, 193, 264.

[20] Larry I. Bland and Sharon Stevens, eds., *The Papers of George Catlett Marshall*, vol. 2, (Baltimore: John Hopkins University Press, 1981), 678.

[21] Jonathan Glancey, 'Goodbye to Berlin,' *Guardian Unlimited*, May 12, 2003, Arts Section. http://www.guardian.co.uk/arts/critic/feature/0,1169,954251,00.html. (accessed December 18, 2005).

[22] PBS Online. 'General Curtis E. LeMay, (1906-1990),' *The American Experience: The Race For The Superbomb*, http://www.pbs.org/wgbh/amex/bomb/peopleevents/pandeAMEX61.html. (accessed September 1, 2005).

[23] *Fog of War - Eleven Lessons from the Life of Robert S. McNamara*, DVD, dir. Errol Morris, 107 min. (New York: Sony Pictures Classics, 2003). T.J. Cronley (Maj.), 'Curtis E. LeMay The Enduring "Big Bomber Man" ' (unpublished report, Command and Staff College Education Center, Quantico, VA), 1986, http://www.globalsecurity.org/wmd/library/report/1986/CTJ.htm. (accessed September 2, 2005).

[24] Benny Doyle Conine Sr. and William Doswell Conine, III, 'Conine Brothers' Early Years,' 2005, unpublished manuscript (photocopy), p. 268, Family Memoirs, The Woodlands, Texas. Milton Garin, e-mail message to author, April 11, 2005.

[25] Herman Wolk, 'The Twentieth Against Japan,' *Air Force Magazine*, April, 2004, 73.

[26] Florio Spero, March 10, 1945.

[27] Milton Garin, e-mail message to author, June 23, 2003.

[28] In a play on words used by Japanese propagandists to portray Allied soldiers as brutal (*kichiku bei-ei* (鬼畜米英), literally 'demon-beast American-British'), LeMay was named *kichiku rumei* (鬼畜ルメイ). The term is still commonly used today by Japanese with ultranationalist views.

[29] *Fog of War.*

[30] Thomas R. Searle, 118.

[31] John W. Dower, *War without Mercy: Race and Power in the Pacific War* (New York: Pantheon, 1986).

[32] Richard Rhodes, 'LeMay's Vision of War'. St. Clair McKelway, *A Reporter with the B-29ers* (New York: New Yorker Magazine, June 23, 1945), 36; quoted in T.J. Cronley.

[33] Florio Spero, March 20, 1945. W.M. Rice, 33. Although the official history for the Sixth Bomb Group, it was written hastily at the end of the war and contains a number of errors or omissions. *Pirate's Log* mistakenly attributes this incident to the crew of a Captain Jones instead of Captain Jordan.

[34] William Conine, e-mail message to author, May 24, 2005.

[35] United States Strategic Bombing Survey, *Effects of Air Attacks on Japanese Urban Economy* (Washington, DC: Government Printing Office, 1947), 29-30.

[36] MacKenzie notes that captured Nazi documents reveal Hitler and Goebbels both encouraged civilians to murder Allied 'terror fliers' shot down in the aftermath of the incendiary attacks on Dresden. As cited in S.P. MacKenzie, 'The Treatment of Prisoners of War in World War II,' *The Journal of Modern History*, 66, no. 3 (September 1994), 494.

[37] Justin McCurry, 'Japan's sins of the past,' *Guardian Unlimited*, October 28, 2004, http://www.guardian.co.uk/elsewhere/journalist/story/0,7792,1338296,00.html. (accessed November 20, 2005)

[38] Chester Marshall & Ray 'Hap' Halloran, *Hap's War: The Incredible Survival Story of a WW II Prisoner of War Slated for Execution* (Collierville, Tennessee: Global Press, 1998), 37-38. Fiske Hanley, *Accused American War Criminal* (Austin, TX: Eakin Press, 1997), 66-70.

[39] Joseph F. McCloskey, 'U.S. Operations Research in World War II,' *Operations Research*, 36, no. 6 (November-December 1987): 912.

[40] T.H. Moorer (Interrogator), 'Interrogation Nav. No. 62. USSBS No. 256. Mine Warfare: Shimonoseki Straits and Formosa Areas (Interrogation of Captain MINAMI, Rokuemon, IJN; with the First Escort Fleet in TAKAO and MOJI, and on the Staff of the Seventh Fleet),' in *United States Strategic Bombing Survey (Pacific): Interrogations of Japanese Officials*, ed. Naval Analysis Division (Washington, D.C.: Naval Analysis Division, 1945), 257, http://www.ibiblio.org/hyperwar/AAF/USSBS/IJO/IJO-62.html. (accessed May 24, 2005). T.H. Moorer (Interrogator), 'Interrogation Nav. No. 26 USSBS No. 103. Mine Warfare (Interrogation of Captain TAMURA, Kyugo, IJN. War time duties were devoted to mine construction and mine sweeping),' in *United States Strategic Bombing Survey (Pacific)*, ed. Naval Analysis Division (Washington, DC.: Naval Analysis Division, 1945), 116, http://www.ibiblio.org/hyperwar/AAF/USSBS/IJO/IJO-26.html. (accessed May 25, 2005). *United States Strategic Bombing Survey, Summary Report (Pacific War)* (Washington, DC: Government Printing Office, 1946), 11-12, http://www.ibiblio.org/hyperwar/AAF/USSBS/PTO-Summary.html#thamotjc/ (accessed May 24, 2005).

[41] *United States Strategic Bombing Survey, Summary Report* (Pacific War) (Washington, DC: Government Printing Office, 1946), 20-22, http://www.ibiblio.org/hyperwar/AAF/USSBS/PTO-Summary.html#thamotjc/ (accessed May 24, 2005).

[42] T.H. Moorer (Interrogator), 'Interrogation Nav. No. 26 USSBS No. 103., 117.

[43] 20th Air Force Headquarters, *Tactical Mission Report (9/10 July to 14/15 August)* (San Francisco: Commanding General, USASTAF, APO 234, 1945), 2.

[44] Florio Spero, May 1, 1945.

[45] Florio Spero, April 12 & April 28, 1945.

CHAPTER THREE

DESPERATE RESISTANCE

Japanese homeland defense began to adjust to the new B-29 tactics. Over the next several months growing numbers of B-29s were shot down and the Jordan Crew's missions became progressively more perilous. On April 8, a Mitsubishi 'Zero' shot out Spero's guns. Moments later, a flak burst nearly breached the aft cabin. Everyone felt fortunate that no one had been injured.[1] During a mission to bomb Kanoya Airfield, Japanese fighters flew above them and dropped phosphorous bombs. Grant remembers how the phosphorous would ignite in the air and trail like glowing fingers that seemed to reach downward for the B-29s. Some of the phosphorous brushed against their B-29 and began burning holes in the hull but, again, everyone returned home safely.[2]

A week later over Nagoya, however, they encountered a large number of fighters waiting at the rendezvous point. The gunners fought hard to keep them at bay and downed two before a 'Zero' came in from below and sprayed their B-29 with 20 mm cannon fire. Because the B-29s had continued to fly without most of their protective armor, the hail of shells penetrated the plane, wounding Wride in his leg and hand.[3] They returned to Iwo Jima after dropping their payload. Wride survived, but the crew noticed that he was never the same after this.

Terror Over Tokyo

The latter part of May 1945 was marked by a series of nighttime incendiary raids over Tokyo. The 6th Bomb Group sustained some of its heaviest casualties of the war during these missions, because Japanese anti-aircraft batteries were ready and waiting for low altitude attacks from the B-29s. On their May 23rd mission to Tokyo, two B-29s near Jordan's plane, flown by Lts. John Boynton and Joseph Snyder, were shot out of the sky.[4] Another B-29 crew under the command of Lt. Sam Parks, who shared a Quonset hut with the enlisted men of the Jordan Crew, flew their crippled plane back to Iwo Jima after their copilot had been killed, another had lost his arm, and a piece of flak had gone through their radar operator's head.[5] The Jordan Crew had become close friends with these crewmen, but they bottled up their grief in order to prepare for the following day, when they knew the same gauntlet of anti-aircraft fire would be waiting for them. Little did they realize that this would be the last mission that the original Jordan Crew would fly together.

May 1945 was the time when a flu epidemic swept through Tinian, and several crews had been unable to fly. McGraw had been trying to stave off the flu, but he became so sick that he had to be sent to the base hospital. Without McGraw, the Jordan Crew would be grounded. Jordan wanted to maintain his crew's mission quota so that they could finish their tour of duty as quickly as possible. He spoke with another Air Commander in his squadron, Capt. Jacob Schad of the B-29 nicknamed 'Jake's Jernt'. Schad's engineer, Lt. Charles Schlosser, had been ill a few days earlier and needed to catch up with the rest of his crew's mission quota so that they could all finish together. Schlosser, who had worked earlier for Boeing and who was well acquainted with the mechanics of the B-29, would fly with the Jordan Crew as a substitute engineer for the next mission. As the Jordan Crew took off for Tokyo on the evening of May 25, they would discover firsthand the importance of Schlosser's expert knowledge.[6]

Blood on the Deck

The industrial facilities that the Jordan Crew was preparing to attack were heavily defended by scores of searchlight and anti-aircraft crews. The Jordan Crew was coming in slow and low under the cover of darkness. All was going well until a few kilometers from their target, when, as Schlosser later wrote, they were caught in a 'flock of searchlights'.[7]

Being discovered by searchlights was a terrifying prospect for the B-29er. At such low altitudes and with the B-29's relative clumsiness, the bombers were easy targets for anti-aircraft crews.[8]

The crew held on as Jordan took evasive actions to somehow escape the lights. All efforts were useless. There was nothing left to do but to finish the mission.

Flak began to pop probingly in the air as the Jordan Crew started their bomb run. Garin transferred targeting and navigation control to Wride, who signaled that the bomb bay doors were coming open. He instructed the designated crewmen to give a visual confirmation that the doors had opened successfully. 'Bombs away,' shouted Wride, as nine thousand kilos of incendiary bombs streaked towards their mark. Flak exploded around their plane, but the crew was unscathed. The Jordan Crew began to gain altitude. The searchlights continued to follow them. Wride announced that the bomb bay doors were closing and transferred navigation control back to Garin, who gave Jordan the headings for their return. Everyone breathed a sigh of relief. Feeling expansive, Garin leaned back in his chair to prop his feet up on the navigator's desk.

Then it happened. Everyone blinked in shock, realizing slowly through the smoke and debris that they had just been hit. Flak had ripped through the plane. Schlosser's engineering station was smashed as he was showered with glass and metal. Wiernik was dumbstruck as flak had narrowly missed him but devastated the radio room. Garin was fortunate, but not quite: He was on the deck holding his foot. He had been hit, but had he not propped up his feet, the flak would have hit him in the head.

The plane reeled as Jordan struggled to get the B-29 under control. Crewmen tried calling over the interphone to find out what had happened, but the flak had knocked the system out of commission. Schlosser pulled off his flak helmet and went to the cockpit. Jordan shouted back that the rudder controls had been damaged. He could keep the plane in the air but couldn't change course. 'And,' Jordan said grimly, 'we're heading back over the target again.'

Searchlights again locked onto the Jordan Crew. They braced themselves for the inevitable. It was as bright as midday in the cabins of the plane. The crew looked at each other quietly and also at the damage inside the plane. Garin was writhing in pain and bleeding profusely.

Somehow, they passed over the target without any more hits. The crew breathed a second sigh of relief as they headed out over the silent darkness of the ocean.

Wiernik and Schlosser dragged Garin over to the engineering station and began to attend to his wounds. Jordan needed to check on his crew and take an inventory of the damage, but Hawkins, who had done little to help Jordan after they had been hit, was now completely unresponsive and staring forward as if in a trance. Jordan put the plane on autopilot and checked on Garin, who was now being bandaged and receiving plasma. He wasn't looking good. In the days of the B-29, pilots were almost entirely dependent upon the constant guidance of the navigator. Without Garin, Jordan was blind. He called down to Wride, still bandaged from his own injuries from earlier, and asked if he could navigate the plane. Wride admitted sheepishly that he didn't have the confidence to do it. [9]

Their situation was serious. The rudder cable had been cut. The radio compass was damaged and they were unable to climb higher to get above the clouds for star navigation. They broke out the magnetic emergency compass, which was inaccurate, but was still able to confirm that they were flying off course. The number two engine had blown its oil line and wasn't working. The pressure line to the rear bomb bay doors had been hit and wouldn't close. The drag from this alone was seriously affecting how much fuel they were expending. Their radio was damaged and the crew couldn't call for help. On top of all of this, the plane just entered a storm and it was raining heavily outside. Jordan took the plane off of autopilot and tried to keep it steady in the turbulence.

Jordan spoke to the crew in the front cabin as he flew the plane, and the message was relayed back to the gunners in the aft cabin by sending a man through the access tunnel. It was up to them to decide. Would they bail out now and hope to be captured by the Imperial Navy, or would they go on until they had to ditch their plane into the ocean? Neither option offered much hope. All quickly came to the decision that if the plane couldn't be repaired, they had a better chance of surviving by bailing out over the ocean, though they knew that even if their location was known by air and sea rescue, many were not found in time. [10]

The crew set themselves to the task of trying to repair the plane. A bit of good news came early: Wiernik announced that he had fixed the radio and had gotten a bearing on their position.

Schlosser crawled through the access tunnel over the bomb bays to attempt repairing the control cable from the aft cabin. In order to access the cable, he discovered that he would have to lie on a 25 centimeter catwalk over the open bomb bay. Because the plane was shaking from the turbulence of the storm, he wouldn't be able to wear his parachute for fear of losing his balance.

Schlosser began to take off his parachute while Grant was sent back to the flight deck to get an emergency release cord that was scavenged from inside the plane, as well as some metal rods that were used for reinforcing the fore cabin. As Grant emerged from the access tunnel over the bomb bays, he noticed that there was trouble in the cockpit. Jordan was trying to keep the plane aloft unassisted and was livid with rage. Hawkins was still sitting in the copilot's seat, staring forward and oblivious to what was going on around him.[11] Wiernik was at his work station, trying to ignore what was happening in the cockpit and shrugging off the realization that, in a few hours, they were probably going to die on the open seas. Garin was groaning with pain.

Over the next hour, Schlosser eventually succeeded in splicing the control cable to the rudder. With the help of the gunners, they bent the ends of the metal rods into hooks, reached down, and pulled the bomb bay doors shut. By this time, Garin was feeling better and asked to be helped back to his station. He gave the vital navigation headings Jordan needed to make it back to Tinian.[12] He put them back on course, and Schlosser, who had also returned to his station, checked what gauges were still operational. He determined they still had enough fuel to return to base. The crew cheered when Wiernik announced that he had made contact with two other B-29s returning from Tokyo. They volunteered to fly ahead of the Jordan Crew and further assist in guiding them to Tinian, just in case Garin lost consciousness.[13]

After landing, Garin was immediately rushed to the hospital and the crew inspected their plane. They found over one hundred holes in the fuselage alone.[14]

Thinking the Unthinkable

Garin survived, but he had lost part of his foot. After a period of recovery on base, the crew was told that he would soon be shipped back to the US. The Jordan Crew's scarred plane was decommissioned and they would have to wait a while before getting a new one. Jordan took advantage of the downtime to hold a party in his Quonset hut. He wanted to allow everyone to blow off steam and to take the edge off of the terror and fatigue of the last mission. By all accounts, they shouldn't have made it back alive. The loss of Garin and the thought of bailing out still weighed heavily on the crew, though no one spoke about it.

As everyone drank deep into the night, someone finally popped the question: What would you have done if we had bailed out over Japan? Everyone had heard about the propaganda broadcasts from Japan describing the execution of downed fliers from the Doolittle Raid. Going down over Japan was a frightening prospect. Garin explained:

> At the time, nobody really knew what happened to crewmen who went down over Japan. Rumors had come back from Japanese POW camps in the Philippines about the Bataan Death March about how they'd treated prisoners, so what little we knew was terrifying. Bailing over Japan was like jumping into a sea of darkness. None of us knew what was waiting for us down there.[15]

35

As each was asked in turn, some, such as Jordan, didn't want to entertain the topic. He sat quietly, nursing his bourbon. Most said they would have taken their chances and surrendered. Wride, however, who was showing signs of battle fatigue after narrowly escaping death a week earlier, said that he would never be taken alive. Spero piped in, saying he would rather go out in a blaze of glory, taking out as many Japanese as he could before they got him. Hawkins spoke as if awakened from a long slumber, and said dolefully that he would never bail out over Japan. Everyone understood what this meant.[16]

Battle Fatigue

For his part in getting the crew back to Tinian, Garin received a Purple Heart and the Silver Star for Bravery. He remained on base for a month, and frequently hobbled around on crutches to talk with the crew. On the day he was being shipped back, Jordan, McGraw and Wride went to see him off. Words were difficult. A silent hug and a pat on the back was all each could muster. As Garin waved goodbye from the deck of the ship, even from this distance all could still feel the weight of what they could not bring themselves to say on the dock. Tragically, for Jordan, Wride and others on the crew, it truly would be their final farewell.[17]

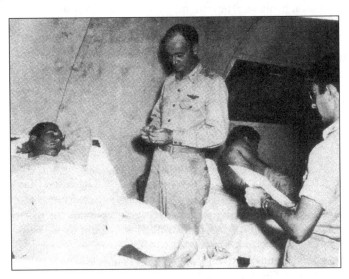

Milton Garin receiving his Purple Heart before returning to the United States. He was not on the Jordan Crew's final mission.
(W.M. Rice, ed., *Pirate's Log: A Historical Record of the Sixth Bombardment Group*, Manila: 2771st Engr. Base Reproduction Co., 1946, 19.)

Like many young soldiers, Garin had been convinced that he would survive the war. He had often told the crew that he was their good luck charm. 'As long as I'm with you, you'll be ok, because I'm going to make it back home, and that means you will too.'[18] And after all they had been through, some on the crew had almost started to believe him. Garin's physical injuries, however, could not compare with the psychological wounds that his loss would have on the crew. It soon became apparent that he had been as important as Jordan for holding the crew together.

In one of the few sociological studies on B-29 crews and their commanders, Robert Hall found that even more than their military prowess or the ability to shepherd a crew, the air commanders who were most successful were those who could foster a personal closeness with each crewman.[19] Jordan had put a high priority on encouraging group camaraderie, and would talk with individuals over drinks at the Officers' Club. But it had been Garin, with his talent for interacting with people on a one-to-one basis, who had served as the unofficial crew counselor and the vital link between the officers and enlisted men.

Now Garin was gone, and with him went Kruvant's main source of emotional support. Kruvant became increasingly terrified during subsequent missions, and trembled violently at his post when they approached the target.[20] Hawkins became distant and unresponsive and Wride quieter. Some of the enlisted men started taking sleeping pills. Jordan's demeanor took a dark and grim turn. He spent less time with the crew on their down time and more with other B-29 air commanders, where he would drink heavily until the early hours. Some of the crew had quietly started to notice that, from time to time, Jordan showed up at early morning missions with a hangover. Their respect for him was such that no one dared speak about this. It was one of their family secrets, and Jordan was always at his best long before they approached the target. Nevertheless, this was one more sign that stress, fear and fatigue were taking a terrible toll on the crew.[21]

A New Navigator and a New Plane

The Jordan Crew needed a new navigator. Garin was replaced by Paul Trump, a college student from Kimberton, Pennsylvania. Trump, who was a friend of Garin, had volunteered for the Army Air Force against the pacifist wishes of his father, who was a Lutheran minister. Trump wanted to fulfill his patriotic duty before returning home to finish college and then going to seminary.

Trump had started his training in radar bombardment. However, they had used antiquated equipment on old sub-chaser planes and timed their drops with stopwatches. He then trained as a B-29 navigator and was transferred to air photo reconnaissance. For a few weeks he flew recon missions over Japan with the 3rd Photo Reconnaissance Squadron stationed on Guam before being transferred to Tinian. The day after Trump had arrived, he was ordered to report to the office of Col. Theodore Tucker. Trump recalls the meeting.

> He [Col. Tucker] had looked over my records and saw that I had radar training. The navigator on the lead crew had his foot shot off and he was assigning me to the lead crew. I repeated the fact that I knew nothing about bombing by radar. 'Well,' he said, 'You have the rating. You'd better learn

by tomorrow morning.' I spent half the night learning on the trainer. I should also state that navigators also received a few practice runs over Truk.[22]

Trump had logged many hours in B-29s navigating from the relative safety of high altitude photo reconnaissance, but this experience was very different from that of guiding the lead plane on radar guided bombing missions. Before Garin returned to the States, Trump told him that he was worried about being unprepared for this new assignment.[23] The Jordan Crew, who had gone to Saipan for a few days of R&R, returned to find their new navigator desperately searching for someone to help him learn how to use B-29 radarscopes. Jordan was not pleased to have received an unproven navigator for his crew. He treated Trump professionally, but was quick to scold when he found Trump struggling with the new equipment.[24] This was unfortunate, because navigation was crucial to the success of missions, and Jordan, as the ranking officer and responsible for the safety of the crew, should have better facilitated Trump's training. In hindsight, after what happened over Tokyo, it is clear that Jordan should have also required that his bombardier sit down and learn how to navigate.

The Jordan Crew in early July.
Back Row (from left to right): McGraw, Spero, unknown trainee, Grant, Wiernik, Adams, Burkle and Kruvant. Front Row (left to right): Hawkins, Wride, Trump and Captain Jordan.
(Photo courtesy of Robert Grant.)

Painful Adjustment Period

The predicament that Trump faced was a common one for replacement crewmen. Sociologist Leonard Berkowitz's study of the cohesiveness of forty-eight B-29 crews found that a crewman's chances for fitting in depended on his willingness to conform to the group's unspoken norms. These were usually set by the air commander.[25] Barring this, a crewman could win the respect of his peers if he was skilled in the technical performance of his duties. Trump faced both challenges. Not only had the Jordan Crew already bonded from the shared experience of over twenty harrowing missions, it was difficult for Trump, who had come from an educated Christian background, to find much in common with most of the men on Jordan's rough, hard-drinking, blue-collar crew. As a replacement crewman, Trump's stayed in a different Quonset hut, which further curtailed the time he could have spent bonding with Jordan, Wride and Hawkins. Even when he had the opportunity, Trump's Christian values precluded him from drinking parties that Jordan was famous for. Nevertheless, Trump had a tremendous amount of respect for Jordan's skill as a pilot and, recognizing Jordan's crew as war weary, he focused on his 'on the job' training.

A Portent of Things to Come

A few days after Trump had joined the crew, they received their third plane, unaware that it had already been nicknamed the *Sharron Linn* by the crew who had flown it to Tinian.[26] Jordan ordered Hawkins to take their new B-29 out for a shakedown flight while most of the crew rested on base. Hawkins hadn't mentioned to anyone that he planned on bringing along a nurse that he had recently met. They flew around for a couple of hours and landed without incident, but when the enlisted men in the aft cabin learned that a woman had been on board, they were shocked and furious. Burkle sputtered, 'That's it. We're done for. The plane's cursed. We'll never make it back home now.'[27] The words had the ring of prophesy when on the following day, Wride was wounded by flak piercing the window of the bombardier's station.[28]

[1] Florio Spero, April 8, 1945, war diary, Spero Family Collection, Homer Glen, Illinois.
[2] Robert Grant, interview by author, April 23, 2004, MD Recording. Florio Spero, May 7, 1945.
[3] Florio Spero, May 15, 1945. W.M. Rice, ed., *Pirate's Log: A Historical Record of the Sixth Bombardment Group* (Manila: 2771st Engr. Base Reproduction Co, 1946), 43.
[4] W.M. Rice, 43.
[5] Florio Spero, May 24, 1945. Sam Parks, interview by author, March 20, 2004, MD Recording. Mysteriously, the copilot had predicted he would be killed only a few days earlier.
[6] Jay Martin, e-mail message to author, September 29, 2006. Martin is the grandson of the late Jacob Schad.
[7] Charles Schlosser, letter to Bernice 'Bunny' Schlosser, May 30, 1945.
[8] Robert Grant, April 23, 2004. Roger Mudd, ann., *Unsung Heroes of the B-29s*, Videocassette, 50 min. (History Channel (A&E Network), 2001).
[9] Milton Garin, e-mail message to author, May 15, 2003.

[10] Robert Grant, interview by author, October 25, 2005, MD Recording.

[11] Robert Grant, October 25, 2005.

[12] Milton Garin, May 15, 2003.

[13] Charles Schlosser, May 30, 1945. 'General Orders #81, Section III.' (San Francisco: Headquarters Twentieth Air Force APO 234, October 2, 1945), 5.

[14] Florio Spero, May 26, 1945.

[15] Milton Garin, interview by author, March 20, 2004, MD Recording.

[16] Edmund Steffler (Capt.), 'Missing Air Crew Report #14786' (College Park, Maryland: NARA, 1945, July 23, photocopied). Milton Garin, e-mail message to author, July 1, 2003.

[17] Milton Garin, interview by author, November 10, 2006, Internet chat transcript.

[18] Milton Garin, interview by author, November 17, 2005, notes.

[19] Robert Hall, 'Social influence on the air commander's role,' *American Sociological Review*, 20, no. 23 (1953), 299.

[20] Robert Grant, October 25, 2005.

[21] Florio Spero, May 27, 1945. Robert Grant, April 23, 2004. Sam Parks, March 20, 2004. Paul Trump, interview by author, May 14, 2003, notes.

[22] Paul Trump, 'War Memories,' 2003, unpublished manuscript (photocopy), 1, Trump Family Papers, Lititz, PA. Paul Trump, e-mail message to author, June 30, 2003. Paul Trump, e-mail message to author, June 23, 2003. Paul Trump, interview by author, September 13, 2004, MD Recording.

[23] Milton Garin, e-mail message to author, May 3, 2007.

[24] Paul Trump, interview by author, March 23, 2004, MD Recording.

[25] Leonard Berkowitz, 'Group Norms Among Bomber Crews: Patterns of Perceived Crew Attitudes, 'Actual' Crew Attitudes, and Crew Liking Related to Aircrew Effectiveness Related to Far Eastern Combat,' *Sociometry*, 19, no. 3 (September, 1956), 152.

[26] This name was still on the records later when the Missing Air Crew Report (MACR) was filed for the Jordan Crew following their failure to return from Niigata. George McGraw, letter to author, June 23, 2003. Florio Spero, May 28, 1945. Edmund Steffler (Capt.), 1.

[27] Paul Trump, March 23, 2004.

[28] Florio Spero, June 5, 1945.

CHAPTER FOUR

JAPAN AND NIIGATA IN 1945

Niigata was one of the major ports officially opened to the West when Japan ended its policy of isolation in the mid-19th Century. Often called the 'water capital' of Japan, Niigata was more of a backwater to the new elites of Tokyo. It had not been forgotten that Niigata had been on the losing side of a civil war that had cost the Imperial Government dearly in late 1868.[1] In later years the people of Niigata had taken a stance that was far more pragmatic. As a city dominated by the old merchant class they shunned tradition and focused on the modest profits that could be made from becoming one of Japan's designated international ports. But the private opinions and personal attitudes that many harbored towards Tokyo and non-Japanese could just as easily have found their equivalent in places such as Mobile, Alabama, or Gulfport, Mississippi. Residents generally appreciated the fact that the forbidding mountain ranges between Niigata and Tokyo had kept them comfortably isolated.

Niigata City by the shores of the Shinano River in the late 1800s.
(Photo courtesy of the Niigata Municipal Department of Cultural History.)

From its humble beginnings as a sleepy seaside town, Niigata grew to be an important port for maintaining the supply lines of the Empire. During the war, and even more so in 1945, cargo ships arrived daily with coal, food, raw materials and passengers from Japan's colonies in Manchuria and Korea. Niigata sits astride the estuaries of two of Japan's largest rivers, the Shinano and the Agano. From here, barges ferried goods and people further inland. The older, central part of the city is actually a small island connected by the Bandai Bridge to the mainland, though at that time many would cross the Shinano by ferry. Like Venice or Bangkok, the old town was criss-crossed with canals that were crowded with boats carrying anything from passengers to pickles.

Niigata's West Port before the beginning of the Second World War.
(Photo courtesy of the Niigata Municipal Department of Cultural History.)

The War Comes to Niigata

In the early days of Operation Starvation, the rise of Niigata as Japan's lifeline to its Northeast Asian colonies was a windfall for the city. All manner of materials flowed through on their way to Tokyo and elsewhere. Special wood pulp out of Sakhalin (then the Japanese territory of Karafuto) was brought to Niigata and made into cards for IBM machines captured in the Philippines. These were vital for Japan's signal intelligence department in their efforts to decode intercepted Allied messages.[2] Coal was shipped in from Manchuria. Korea was a major supplier of rice. At this time, even Allied POWs who slaved on the docks of the Marutsu Company as stevedores were able to steal fruit, vegetables, and sometimes seafood.[3]

However, US air reconnaissance had discovered Niigata's new importance by late April 1945. B-29s from the 6th and 9th Bombardment Groups began bearing down on Niigata's harbor by early May 1945.[4]

From an American military point of view the first mining missions to Niigata were unsuccessful. Navigators reported that Niigata's harbor was difficult to approach and there were few reference points that could be used for radar targeting.[5] Niigata's bay is shallow and mines often washed up on the beach or fell inland along the harbor.[6] From the viewpoint of the residents of Niigata, May 1945 was when the war truly became a reality. All through that month, several ships, including a ferry taking passengers to Sado Island, were severely damaged by mines.[7] It is uncertain whether the story comes from local folklore or is an actual occurrence, but older residents of Niigata often speak of a group of boys who had found one of these early mines on the beach. They were blown to pieces either after starting to play with it or trying to take it apart for the metal, which was in short supply due to wartime rationing.[8] After this reported event, whenever mines landed inland, Allied POWs from Niigata Camp 5B were forced to clear them away.[9]

As the mining of Niigata's harbor continued, more ships began to go down, with a commensurate loss of life. The first such incident took place on June 8, 1945, when thirteen crewmen went down with a mail ship. The most tragic sinking took place two weeks before Jordan's plane was shot down. On July 2 a late afternoon ferry owned by Niigata Iron Works was carrying workers and schoolchildren home to the old town side of the city. It was hit by a mine that had floated up the brackish waters of the Shinano delta during high tide. The ferry sank quickly, killing twenty-eight in all. Among the dead was a camp guard from Niigata POW 15B who, had he survived, would have been tried for war crimes.[10] Many who died that day were children on their way home from school.[11] This incident only served to reinforce the wartime depiction of B-29 crewmen as 'demonic beasts' (*kichiku bei-ei*).

Mining drastically cut the amount of food and supplies coming through Niigata, and conditions in the city began to mirror those in other parts of Japan already affected by Operation Starvation. Fishing boats did not dare venture out. Basic medicines became scarce and residents watched helplessly as family members died from treatable illnesses. Women ceased to menstruate and mothers ran dry of milk. Homes became uncharacteristically unkempt as women spent most of their time looking for food.[12]

Food, or the lack of it, became an obsession. Memories of hunger are foremost in the minds of local residents who lived through those days. The average caloric intake fell to about eighty percent of what was needed for basic daily activities.[13] People competed, sometimes brutally, against each other in order to feed their own immediate families. Stealing, dealing on the burgeoning black market, and a shocking level of rude disregard for strangers became commonplace. What food they could get usually consisted of undercooked beans, starchy foods or other 'filling' fare, such as a blue paste called *kōriyan*, all of which were of negligible nutritional value. Morale among the general populace plummeted from the physical exhaustion brought on by a poor diet.

As springtime came to a close in 1945, anthropologist Frederick Hulse, who conducted a number of studies on Japanese society immediately after the war, found that nearly half of the population in Japan no longer believed that the war could be won. The distressing symptoms of malaise Hulse described had become commonplace.

> Everyone expressed the most loyal of sentiments, not only to the police, but to one another. Yet nothing worthwhile could any longer be accomplished. The most essential repairs could no longer be made. Even trains ran behind schedule – something previously unthinkable.[14]

With the approaching rainy season, a heavy gloom had descended over the city. The grey skies only deepened the feelings of exhaustion, hunger, bitterness, and powerlessness. This was a far cry from the heady, early years of the Empire, when everyone believed with certainty that Japan had finally become a nation of the first rank.

Street scene of downtown Niigata during the summer of 1945.
(Photo courtesy of the Niigata Municipal Department of Cultural History.)

Humble Origins

Japan's rise on the world stage, as well as its love-hate relationship with the West, had started sixty years earlier during the tumultuous era of Emperor Meiji (Mutsuhito) in the late 1800s. It was a time when the western imperial powers were competing in a grab for colonies and natural resources. Asia was theirs for the taking, and Japan could no longer keep the outside world at bay. However,

Japan was still locked in sporadic feudal warfare that erupted between the rival samurai clans who had deposed the Tokugawa Shogunate. Western countries supplied weapons and other material resources, often to both sides in order to hedge their bets. An example of this can be seen during a phase of Japan's civil war in 1868 known as the Boshin War. The Imperial forces received Anglo-American support in the form of finances, advisors and military hardware. The newly-formed Northern Confederacy (*ōetsu reppan dōmei*), of which Niigata, then known as Echigo, was an active member, also received limited, though unofficial, American support.[15] Confidential contacts were equally telling. The imperial forces had Britain's Thomas Glover, who provided a wide selection of arms, while the Northern Confederacy relied on Dutch gunrunners of the likes of the colorful 'General' Eduard Schnell.[16]

Western interests profited handsomely regardless of who won in Japan's political strife, a fact that was not lost on the new order following the Northern Confederacy's crushing defeat. Although the West was respected for its technological superiority, it was feared in equal measure for its sheer military power, willingness to use gunboat diplomacy, and its propensity for playing both sides of Japanese internal problems. The late 1800s was a cruel and pitiless world, but the Meiji oligarchs (*genrō*) were determined not to lose their way of life to the foreign barbarians.

Forming a Consensus for a Modern State

The samurai class had political influence and military might, but lacked money. The merchant class and industrial and commercial conglomerates (*zaibatsu*) had this in ample supply, but had been excluded from the corridors of power. The dominant warrior clans and major *zaibatsu* came together ostensibly to strengthen Japan's defenses against any plans the West might have had of doing to Japan what it had already done to China and Southeast Asia. These disparate groups, together with intellectuals and bureaucrats, nevertheless came to the table with different agendas. The xenophobic samurai clans, especially the Satsuma and Chōshu, motivated by feudal concepts of conquest, glory and honor, and inflamed as they were by the influx of western military technology centuries ahead of what had been available to them only a few decades earlier, sought military parity with the West. There also was the need for modern weaponry that could be manufactured in Japan and thus end their dependence upon western arms merchants.[17] The *zaibatsu* of Mitsui, Mitsubishi, Sumitomo and others saw great opportunities for increased profits, and along the way, of developing Japan into a trading nation roughly along the lines of Great Britain. Intellectuals sought the introduction of 'enlightened' western ideals such as democracy and social welfare, while preserving the best of Japanese traditions. Centralized control for the orderly running of society was a concern of the bureaucrats and militarists alike.[18]

The Meiji leaders eventually came to the type of pragmatic compromise that is still seen in Japanese society today. Japan would become a modernized society with traditional values. Japan would strive to master western arts and technology while still holding on to a distinctly Japanese identity (*wakon yōsai*), an identity that would be carefully crafted and defined by the elites.[19]

Japan cobbled together European examples for the development of a modern state. Its constitution followed that of Bismarck's Germany, for this provided the oligarchs with centralized control and kept feudal lords in the upper echelons of political power. At the same time, the appearance of a British-style parliamentary system was adopted, offering a 'morning coat' (*mōningu*) – a cloak – of democracy to satisfy intellectuals and the educated lower classes.[20]

'A Wealthy Nation with a Strong Army'

Historian Patrick Smith observed that, 'while Japan was busy westernizing, it was also busy 'samuraizing'.'[21] The military was dominated by the samurai clans who had ousted the Tokugawa Shogunate, but these were too few in number to man a large standing military force. Universal conscription meant that the new armed forces would be built on the backs of farmers and peasants, who gained immediate respectability from their families and peers, since it was believed that they too were now fighting in the spirit of the samurai. The infantry discarded an earlier French model for the Prussian military structure, since they were judged as possessing the world's best army following their victory over France in the Franco-Prussian War. The navy received their training and support from the British, who were accepted as having the world's finest fleet during the late 19th century.[22]

Leaders such as Hirobumi Itō, the framer of Japan's Meiji constitution, were convinced that economic wealth and national defense were inseparable. Therefore, Japan would become a nation of commerce and manufacturing (*shōkō rikkoku*) that would strengthen the military. This was expressed in one of the many governmental slogans of those days as *fukoku kyōhei*: 'A Wealthy Nation with a Strong Army'.[23]

The *zaibatsu* and members of the merchant class were soon busily engaged in starting Japan's industrial revolution. Factories and heavy industries began to spread across the country. Oil was discovered in Niigata and small companies owned by wealthy landowners sprang up, but were all eventually consolidated by the government into Niigata Oil (Niigata Jinzo Sekiyū). Niigata Iron Works was started in 1895 and became a major producer in Northern Japan.[24] During most of the Meiji era, however, with the exception of a lonely British consulate and a couple of small German companies, Niigata saw very little in the way of international trade through its ports.[25]

The corporations in Niigata and elsewhere, in association with the *zaibatsu*, had the inside track for lucrative government contracts. They were not completely independent from the government, which both financed and would control key industries through the *zaibatsu*. Neither, however, was the government free from *zaibatsu* influence. In the process, both became inextricably linked with the imperial elites' common goal of building a strong military, industrializing, and securing the material resources that Japan needed to become self–sufficient. Over time, the *zaibatsu* embedded within their corporate structures a culture of 'managerial familism' that would be vital in the Empire's ability to control and mobilize the Japanese people for total warfare.[26]

The lonely courtyard of Niigata's Customs and Immigration Port in 1878. Niigata was an international port in name only until the early Taisho Era. (Photo courtesy of the Niigata Municipal Department of Cultural History.)

Nationalistic Myths

To avoid another civil war, political leaders and intellectuals came together to develop a means for unifying the fractious nation and instilling within the people a Japanese national ethos. State religions in Europe were seen as an important tool used by national politicians for creating such a common identity and for rallying people around a national cause. Over the course of the late 19th and early 20th centuries a uniquely Japanese civil religion that focused on Emperor worship was manufactured from the ideological materials at hand: Japanese Neo-Confucian fundamentalism, the veneration of ancestors and Shinto myths.[27] Where before there had been greater personal loyalty to one's family, clan or fiefdom, historian Carol Gluck writes that the Emperor now had become 'the center of the light of empire [and] the symbol of victory and world power.'[28]

As head of state, the Emperor was, at least formally, the sole authority over the military. However, much of the real power was administrated by a small number of ranking generals, who were some of the select few who had direct access to the Chrysanthemum Throne. Moreover, the Japanese were taught to believe that they were a national family (*kazoku kokka*) and that the Emperor was their father from whom flowed the mystic embodiment of their national essence (*kokutai*). Through the Emperor they were all sons and daughters of that divine character.[29] Japan's leaders, under the Emperor, were the stern elder brothers who administered his will in a spirit of firmness mixed with benevolence.[30]

The educational system discouraged critical discourse and analytical thinking in favor of rote learning and the acquisition of technical skills that would help Japan to catch up with the West. Students wore Prussian-style school uniforms and underwent the mental and physical training necessary to prepare them for military life. Education was centered around the Imperial Rescript on Education, which students recited regularly and were required to memorize. This taught them, among other things, that the Emperor was good, and that they should be faithful and true to the throne as well as to their parents. They should devote themselves to learning arts, technical skills, and to be good, unselfish citizens who were prepared to die defending the Empire. Later, under General Sadao Araki, Japan's Education Minister in the 1930s, schools at all levels became little more than hothouses for militaristic indoctrination. Concepts such as the 'imperial way' (*kōdō*), 'Japanism' (*nippon-shugi*), the 'national essence' (*kokutai*) of the Emperor and the glorification of war were among the many nationalistic themes emphasized in both school ceremonies and curricula.[31]

Early Expansion

It was within this ideological framework that Japan rapidly began to carve out an empire in Asia, starting first with an intimidating use of its own version of gunboat diplomacy with Korea, Formosa (Taiwan) and China in the 1870s, and then followed by the imposition of trade agreements that flooded Northeast Asia with Japanese goods.[32] Okinawa was invaded and claimed for the Empire. Soon afterwards, in the Sino-Japanese War of 1895, China was decisively defeated and Japan won Formosa as a colony and established a number of footholds on the continent. Korea was isolated as the Chinese regional sphere of influence began to contract. Fifteen years later Korea would be annexed outright and incorporated as part of Greater Japan.

The Sino-Japanese War was a prime example of how the *zaibatsu* worked in tandem with the military. Major shipping companies provided transport for troops to the front. The technology and new skills discovered for the development of increasingly advanced weaponry for the Japanese military killed several birds with one stone. The *zaibatsu* fulfilled their obligations to the government by equipping the military, who in turn would open the doors for increased economic expansion, quite literally at gunpoint. The advances in production technology during wartime were then applied to civilian and commercial-based factories in peacetime to increase Japan's manufacturing capabilities both within the Empire and abroad.[33]

This arrangement had not yet reached the smaller *zaibatsu* and corporations in Niigata. They would not have long to wait, however, for additional wars were rapidly appearing on the horizon.

Economically and militarily strategic territories in China were lost during several years of diplomatic wrangling with Russia, thus setting the stage for the Russo-Japanese War. Japan framed this as a defense against Russian encroachment, and in a move that was to be a harbinger of Pearl Harbor, Japanese torpedo boats attacked the unsuspecting Russian fleet docked at Port Arthur during an early morning raid without making a formal declaration of war.[34] Niigata became an important staging platform, and citizens cheered from the city's docks as the Imperial Navy steamed out of West Port and onwards to stunning victories on the high seas. The Japanese navy made good use of its British training. During the Battle of Tsushima, Russian fleet reinforcements were decimated.

Japan's military advances on land were also impressive, but soon became bogged down in the horrors of trench warfare, similar to what would be seen in Europe a few years later. Russian soldiers were the first western people to witness the ferocity of banzai charges, which were ordered by General Maresuke Nogi during the ground offensive on Port Arthur. The result, over twenty-thousand dead and injured, was such that even Emperor Meiji was shocked.[35]

The physical and financial cost of the Russo-Japanese war began to mount, but the military had already devised an exit strategy. Japan approached America to mediate a settlement. By this time Russia was more than willing to negotiate a quick end to the war. It was widely recognized that Japan had won, and pundits at the time predicted that the Empire would be safe from foreign attack for at least fifty years.[36]

Unsuspecting Allies

During these two wars, Japanese leaders had continued to develop the ultranationalist ideology of protecting Japan from western imperialists and of achieving personal glory through sacrificing one's life for the Emperor. A famous example in peacetime came when Emperor Meiji died in 1912. General Nogi, being from the old school of military commanders, demonstrated his remorse for displeasing the Emperor at Port Arthur by committing ritual suicide. Such sacrifices were expected for anyone who was a soldier in the service of the Emperor. During the final days of the Russo-Japanese War, Baron Kentaro Kaneko wrote:

> We fear death just as much as the Western people, but we fear the death of our nation more than we fear individual death. We consider that the death most to be dreaded would be submission to the yoke of the Muscovite. It is patriotism pure and true which makes the Japanese die gallantly. Moreover, we have an old maxim that 'A man lives only one life-time, but his name shall live forever.' We believe that to die on the battlefield for a righteous cause and for the Emperor is the noblest death man can have.[37]

America and Britain viewed these attitudes as sometimes quaint, at other times noble, especially since it had been their Russian rival who had borne the brunt of their Asian understudy.[38] However, the xenophobia which had propelled Japan's leaders to keep the Western world at bay through the creation of an

Asian colonial buffer zone had also already put the Empire on a collision course with the Americans and British. General Gentaro Kodama, a career military officer in both the Sino-Japanese and Russo-Japanese wars, remarked in an address on colonial development while he was Governor General of Taiwan in 1900:

> In recent years, the European powers have expanded their influence in Asia. How should we meet this threat? The military strength of the West is derived from their science and knowledge. For this reason the Western powers have been able to oppress the peoples of the Far East. In order for us to acquire the power to oppose them so that we can continue to dominate in the Far East and preserve the peace, there is no other recourse open to us but to acquire more knowledge and increase our wealth. A country will surely suffer defeat if this is not so. We may speak of economic warfare today as being war waged from the standpoint of economic power.[39]

Such views seemed to have been largely ignored, and Japan proved to be a helpful ally during the First World War, where it had taken German outposts in the South Pacific and China. In the case of China, a nominal ally of Germany, these gains took place in spite of the fact that it had declared itself neutral.

The Empire at High Tide

Japan was in ascendance at the end of the First World War. It had gained new territories with a minimal loss of life and was now one of the Big Five at the new League of Nations. In Niigata and elsewhere, the Empire's military and economic accomplishments were a source of great national pride. It felt good to be on the winning side, and to be a citizen of the Great Japanese Empire. Japan's territories stretched from the Kuriles to Korea, and from Taiwan to the Pescadores. While America and Europe rebuilt their merchant fleets, Japan's vessels and industries had been untouched by the war, thus giving it a new advantage in international trade and commerce.[40]

A Brief Respite: The Taisho Democracy

Times were changing after the 'war to end all wars', during what was later to be called Japan's 'Taisho Democracy'. Named after Meiji's successor, Emperor Taisho (Yoshihito) was not the man his father was. He suffered from poor health and habits of the type that required keeping him behind closed doors. This robbed the military of a powerful symbol and provided an opportunity for liberal thinkers who envisaged a new direction for Japan. In their view, it had been democratic nations who had won the war. For Japan to survive the turn of history, it too must adopt a more democratic stance. Their pro-western, reformist leanings opened new doors for sweeping, though temporary, changes in Japanese society. Public protest was allowed, universal suffrage for men was passed, and aspects of Marxist thinking from the new Soviet Union found its way into some industries in an effort to improve the lot of workers. Pacifism, which had always been a concern of small religious groups such as the Jehovah's Witnesses or the Japanese Non-Church Movement (*mukyōkai*), was now taken up by the *zaibatsu*, who had profited greatly from the First World War.[41]

As the last of the Meiji oligarchs passed away, the *zaibatsu* used their financial resources to purchase political clout. Political parties abounded, though most were viewed by the public as being in the pockets of different business interests. The new line was that war was bad for business, an attitude that was even expressed by some leading officers. In what was interpreted at the time as a remarkable about face, military strategist Matsui Iwane wrote in 1923: 'We must substitute economic cooperation for military invasion, financial influence for military control, and achieve our goals under the slogans of co-prosperity and co-existence, friendship, and cooperation.'[42]

Niigata's bustling Honcho Market during the early Taisho Era.
(Photo courtesy of the Niigata Municipal Department of Cultural History.)

Especially in the major cities, affluence and relaxed attitudes towards traditional values were seen as evidence that Japan had made a break with the ennui of the East, and that it was on its way to achieving the ideals of a Western society. Niigata benefited from the change in government policy. Local museums, somewhat idealistically, portray Niigata's development during these times as *nigiyakana* – lively. More schools and colleges were built. The iron works and oil industry were modernized. A petrochemical port was established. Everywhere were the signs of industry, innovation and affluence. Goods from the colonies flowed to the rest of Japan through Niigata's ports. When Niigata residents talk about the good old days, they usually refer to the fleeting Indian Summer of Taisho.[43]

Dreams of Freedom Fade

The reasons why the Taisho Democracy came to a sudden end are even today a topic of considerable discussion within academic circles. While no one factor exists that can be seen as the primary cause, a number of events conspired against Japan's experiment with a more liberal form of governance. Japan's relationship with America began to sour early on, first by protectionist measures designed to curb Japanese imports, later through trade negotiations that put Japan at a disadvantage, and then finally by racist policies that disallowed Japanese immigration to the United States by placing them on the same list as other 'undesirables' such as Chinese, anarchists, prostitutes, lunatics and the mentally-challenged.[44] The Tokyo Earthquake of 1923, in which over 100,000 died in the resultant fires that swept through the city, had a profound destabilizing effect upon that generation, even as it served as the inspiration for later attacks by LeMay. The Great Depression debilitated the *zaibatsu* and the populace heaped abuse on them for the subsequent economic problems and ruined lives left in its wake. The influence of the *zaibatsu* in government waned as a result and the voices of militarists began to gain currency in society once more.

Some of the early firebrands were veterans of the Russo-Japanese War who had risen through the ranks to become mid-level officers. These and others who followed later, were often from uneducated, impoverished farming backgrounds. They did not fully appreciate foreign concepts such as democracy, and saw Japan as becoming a decadent, dissipated society because of western ideas. For them, Japan was at its best when engaged in glorious conquests for the Emperor.[45] Even before the death of Taisho in 1926, his son Hirohito, as Prince Regent, had already been actively engaged in affairs of state because of his father's slow, withering illness. Young, active and articulate, Hirohito would prove to be suitably (though not always easily) bendable to the military's plans for bringing all of Asia under one roof (*hakko ichiu*).

In the final analysis, it is a common feature in Japanese society not to replace the old with the new, but instead to add the new to the old. Earlier precedents are rarely discarded. Taisho was built on top of Meiji. In the minds of many politicians even during the time of Taisho, allowing universal suffrage for men was less intended to allow the individual exercise of one's political voice, and more to elicit gratitude from the populace, which in turn would result in more men wanting to devote their lives for the Empire.[46] During the last year of Taisho, the Peace Preservation Act (*chian ijihō*) was passed in an effort to fine or imprison leftists or pacifists caught fomenting protest and spreading 'dangerous thoughts'. This law would be 'strengthened' three years later to make unauthorized thinking punishable by life imprisonment or death. Thousands of students, academics and free-thinkers would be imprisoned, but none were executed.[47] School textbooks during the Taisho era still focused on Japan's victories in its previous wars and revered the ashes of warriors that were kept at the Imperial War Shrine at Yasukuni. And while efforts to improve the lives of workers had taken place in some quarters, the financial clout of the *zaibatsu* had kept most attempts at significant reforms to a minimum. The typical work day changed little, and indeed for many it became worse from an overzealous application of scientific management. In addition, the military still lay outside the control of the civil government. As the militarists' influence grew, two competing governments emerged (*nijū seifu*), one civil and one military, which acted under the guise of following the will of the Emperor.

Niigata's West Port during the early Showa Era.
(Photo courtesy of the Niigata Municipal Department of Cultural History.)

As Taisho faded and Hirohito became the Showa Emperor, the militarists enforced their shadow government through the assassinations of business leaders, politicians and premiers who stood in the way of Japan's manifest destiny to rule Asia.[48]

Fascism Within and Conflict Abroad

It was not long before Japan was once again involved in a war of aggression against China. The *zaibatsu* had been brought to heel by the militarists even as they themselves had started to recognize the need for new resources and economic opportunities abroad, mainly because of the setbacks caused by the depression. These could be gained most quickly by militaristic expansion. Companies and factories became the first front for mobilizing the Japanese workforce for war.

The only contemporary example that resembles the rhetoric, social control, and raw indoctrination that pervaded Japan in the beginning years of the Showa Era would be present-day North Korea.[49] Ideologically, as one Japanese writer put it, the country entered 'an enormous black box.'[50] Everywhere, in the temple, at work, in the newspapers and on the radio, the principle was reinforced that doing what you were told without question and trusting your benevolent leaders were vital for keeping one's heart pure and making Japan a stable, harmonious society. Doing things on your own and not cooperating with the flow of society was seen as selfishness, which was perhaps the most shameful thing that could be said about someone.

All true Japanese, regardless of whether they wielded a rifle or a hammer, were told that they were warriors (*kokumin kaihei*). All faithful Japanese were required to make sacrifices and to do their best to keep the homeland safe and strong from foreign imperialists. The best way to keep Japan safe was to fight chaos abroad before it would have to be fought at home. Large numbers of men from Niigata were conscripted and sent off to fight in Manchuria, believing they were working for the greater good of Asia. One old soldier remembers:

> At the time of the Manchurian Incident in 1931, we felt Japan should go out there and use Japanese technology and leadership to make China a better country. What was happening on the battlefield was all secret then, but I felt sure that the Greater East Asia Co-Prosperity Sphere would be of crucial importance to the backward races. Japan and Germany would only have to combine forces to break the Anglo-Saxon hold on Asia, and redistribute the colonies. That's how we felt then.[51]

Yet the Empire's leadership during Showa was often opaque to the Japanese people. After early gains, the war in China became a quagmire. Citizens were sometimes told the second Sino-Japanese conflict was a war against communism, and other times that it was Japan's war against western imperialism. Japan's new pact with Germany was ironic in that while Nazi Germany was supporting Chiang Kai-shek, the Japanese Imperial army was fighting his troops in the field. Its alliance with world fascism and Japan's rapid expansion in Asia put the Empire further at odds with America and Britain. The military on both sides had believed for years that war was unavoidable. Yet even as Japan's civil government was attempting to work out a peaceful settlement for the growing tensions between America and Japan, the military had already set its secret plans for Pearl Harbor into motion. During the confusion of these times, many Japanese were never really certain what they were fighting for, except that whatever happened, it was hoped that Japan would eventually rest secure from the threats of a wild and frightening world. In 1941, Takao Okuna expressed the first feelings that many had during the early days of the ill-fated 'Pacific War':

> The attitudes of ordinary people, who had felt ambivalent about the war against China, and even of intellectuals who denounced it as an invasion, were transformed as soon as the war against Britain and the U.S. began…there was a sense of euphoria that we'd done it at last; we'd landed a punch on those arrogant great powers Britain and America, on those white fellows. As the news of one victory after another came in, the worries faded, and fear turned to pride and joy…All the feelings of inferiority of a colored

people from a backward country, towards white people from the developed world, disappeared in that one blow…Never in our history had we Japanese felt such pride in ourselves as a race as we did then.[52]

Those with experience abroad, however, knew that a war with America would be foolhardy at best and suicidal at worst. Toshio Yoshida, a young lieutenant attached to the Intelligence Department of the Imperial Navy General Staff, recalls that day when Pearl Harbor was attacked. 'I felt like someone had poured cold water on my head. I knew Japan shouldn't fight a war. I looked at Japan like an outsider…people like me thought from the beginning that Japan would be completely defeated.'[53]

Disappointment and Growing Resentment in Niigata

Such were the events that had placed Niigata citizens in the depressing situation that they were facing by mid-1945. Radio broadcasts continued to report on Japanese victories and of valiant resistance from unseen battlefields, but everyone realized from the military's inability to down even one of the B-29s criss-crossing Niigata's night-time skies, the growing deprivation, sunken ships in their harbors, stories from displaced family members about the horrors of the Tokyo fire-bombings, reports of colonies in the South Pacific being occupied and of staggering losses on Okinawa, that Japan was losing the war – badly.[54]

Conflict simmered under the thin veneer of social harmony. The upper classes felt as if they were no longer being afforded the respect due to their position in society. The poor would appear friendly to the military, but unless there was some personal family connection, privately many felt contempt for the military's incompetence and overbearing manner. The Imperial Government had conducted several studies and was well aware of this disgruntlement. They feared that the people were losing the will to fight on.[55]

The situation was untenable, and some in the government wanted Japan to sue for peace. The Emperor himself, though early on a willing participant in the plans to expand the Empire, also expressed, in a dissembling manner, his wishes for a speedy conclusion of the war.[56] However, the militarist radicals who had seized power in the years leading up to the war were calling the shots. For them the die had been cast. The people needed to be kept in line if the country was going to survive. This war had been framed as Japan's struggle against cold, Caucasian imperial powers. Generals such as Curtis LeMay taught them that there would be no mercy when these soldiers came. Better to die fighting for one's beliefs than to suffer the ignominy of living as slaves of the white man. Hanama Tasaki describes the mental state of many trapped in this ideological morass of their own making. 'They had the courage to charge a thousand enem[ies], but not the determination to stand up for a single right.'[57]

Increasing numbers of recruits that could have been sent to the battle front were instead sent to the Military Police (kempei-tai) for the purpose of stifling discontent. Together with the government's network of informants (jikei-dan), they spied on the people, and were quick to react if anyone openly criticized the government or expressed unpatriotic sentiment. Exceptions were usually made for those who had lost family members in the incendiary attacks. Normally the local police would look the other way for a few days after the funeral. But if someone continued to foment unrest they were referred to the *kempei-tai* so that their dangerous thoughts could be rectified by 'coercive measures.'[58] In a very real sense, the citizens of Niigata had become prisoners in their own country.

It was within this environment that surviving Niigata residents saw themselves as victims of the war, a sentiment that has ironic parallels with the feelings of many former Allied POWs, and other Asian peoples who themselves suffered under the Japanese Empire. In places like Niigata people could only focus on their own hardships. Why and how they had gotten into their present situation was less clear. Men who returned from the front in China didn't talk about the war. Why would any man want to tell his family about what he had seen and done there? Those sent to the war in the Pacific rarely came back at all. Women and children knew only the hunger, loss and hopelessness of their daily lives. They had been taught to depend on others within a group for help and direction. Nowhere had any been told that one person could make a difference. Takehiko Fukunaga, a young man about to be sent off to war, expresses the private feelings that many felt during that summer of 1945.

> A solitary person cannot do a thing even if he dislikes this war...If there were some kind of organization where all the people would oppose the war could get together and stop these hostilities, I would gladly participate. I would throw away my tiny solitude and fight for the happiness of all. But where can I find such an organization? I do not know a thing about one...in a country where powerful military-police politics has been generated, any sprout of freedom, no matter how infinitesimal, is lopped off instantly.[59]

Without such groups to join, however, the only option was to continue fighting. Masao Shirakawa recalls the attitude of the people in Niigata that summer, just before he himself was sent to Korea to begin his training as a kamikaze pilot.

> We knew we had lost the war, and that our leaders had made a terrible mistake. No one dared talk about it, but we all knew, just by looking at each other. But we were all still ready to fight and die – not for the Emperor or anything like that – we were ready to die to save our families. We hoped that our deaths would somehow save Japan from being destroyed.[60]

In a spirit of heroic stoicism, learned helplessness, or perhaps a mixture of both, Niigata citizens muttered *shikata ga nai* (there's nothing we can do about it) and continued to press forward with preparations for the land defense of the home islands, the decisive operation (*ketsu-gō sakusen*) that would hopefully force the Americans to a negotiated truce. Little did the inhabitants know that they were living under a secret and particularly gruesome sentence. In May 1945 the Atomic Targeting Committee working for US War Secretary Henry L.

Stimpson nominated three Japanese cities which had the required characteristics of overall size, flatness and population density suitable for an atomic attack. The cities were, in order, Kyoto, Hiroshima and Niigata. Each of these had been quarantined from any conventional attack to allow the effects of the A-bomb to be accurately measured on a pristine target.

Kyoto, the ancient capital of Japan and a cultural jewel which today has many World Heritage listings, was preferred by the US military for the cultural shock which would accrue from its destruction. Fortunately, in June 1945, Kyoto was saved by Stimpson, who had spent his honeymoon there. The list was expanded to include Kokura, and by July, Nagasaki had also been added. As the clock ticked on towards the climax of the Second World War, the dawn of the nuclear era, Niigata and the other three atomic target cities grew increasingly restless. People often whispered to each other, 'Why hasn't Niigata been firebombed yet? When are we going to get hit?'[61]

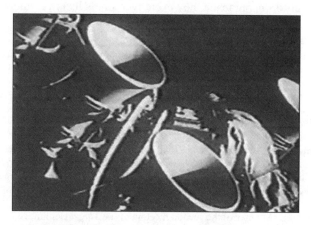

Japanese Searchlight Team. The 'war tubas' would listen for the frequency of B-29 engines. With luck, searchlight teams could pinpoint the B-29s overhead. (NARA.)

Niigata's Anti-aircraft Defenses

When B-29s began mining Niigata's harbors, veterans from the campaign in China who had returned to Niigata were called up to form anti-aircraft units. The first emplacements were set up on the sandy hills above the side of the old town that looked over the Sea of Japan.[62] This was a logical place to start, since the same location had been used in the late 1800s as a cannon emplacement for guarding against possible foreign incursions, when international intrigue suggested that Great Britain was casting envious eyes upon Niigata's harbors as a potential base for Northeast Asian commerce.[63]

These first anti-aircraft squads were unable to stop the B-29s from mining the harbors because the planes came in one at a time in the dead of night, dropped their mines, and then flew off as quickly as possible. The undersides of the planes were painted black, making it even more difficult for searchlights to spot them in the evening sky.[64]

In June 1945, seasoned anti-aircraft units were transferred to Niigata from Tokyo.[65] These troops had considerably more experience with downing B-29s and were equipped with searchlight crews that used listening devices and rudimentary radar.[66] American intelligence realized this when searchlight crews in Niigata began tracking B-29s even when they were above the thick, low cloud cover that hangs over the city during the rainy season. Intelligence also revealed that anti-aircraft units had been trained in new tactics by German specialists and as a result, their accuracy had improved dramatically.[67]

Despite all of this, the anti-aircraft batteries in Niigata continued to have trouble targeting the B-29s mining their waters. This was partly due to the aircrews' tactic of dropping thin strips of aluminum (called 'rope' by B-29 crewmen). This effectively jammed the radar-guided searchlights.[68]

As July 19 approached, however, everyone's luck was about to change.

---

[1] In fact, Niigata had come close to defeating the Imperial Army on several occasions, had rebel forces been better supplied. As cited in Harold Bolitho, 'The Echigo War (1868),' *Monumenta Nipponica*, 34, no. 3 (Autumn 1979), 259-277.

[2] Louis Allen, 'Japanese Intelligence Systems,' *Journal of Contemporary History*, 22, no. 4 (October 1987), 557.

[3] Leonard Robinson, *Forgotten Men* (Victoria, BC: Trafford, 2002), 91-94. Harold Angus Martin Atkinson, interview by Charles G. Roland, MD, May 27, 1983, interview HCM 7-83, transcript, Oral History Archives Hannah Chair for the History of Medicine, McMaster University, Hamilton, Ontario. Isaac Freisen, *Experiences as a Prisoner-of-War 1941-1945*, interview by Charles G. Roland, M.D, March 9, 1985, interview HCM 26-85, transcript, Oral History Archives Hannah Chair for the History of Medicine, McMaster University, Hamilton, Ontario.

[4] Target Committee, 'Minutes of the second meeting of the Target Committee Los Alamos' US National Archives, Record Group 77, Records of the Office of the Chief of Engineers, Manhattan Engineer District, TS Manhattan Project File '42-'46, folder 5D Selection of Targets, 2 Notes on Target Committee Meetings, May 10, 1945), http://www.childrenofthemanhattanproject.org/HISTORY/H-07d.htm. (accessed September 4, 2005). Niigata City Historical Board, 78.

[5] 20th Air Force Headquarters, *Tactical Mission Report (9/10 July to 14/15 August)* (San Francisco: Commanding General, USASTAF, APO 234, 1945), 5.

[6] T.H. Moorer (Interrogator), 'Interrogation Nav. No. 26 USSBS No. 103. Mine Warfare (Interrogation of Captain TAMURA, Kyugo, IJN. Wartime duties were devoted to mine construction and mine sweeping),' in *United States Strategic Bombing Survey (Pacific)*, ed. Naval Analysis Division (Washington, DC: Naval Analysis Division, 1945), 116-117, http://www.ibiblio.org/hyperwar/AAF/USSBS/IJO/IJO-26.html. (accessed May 25, 2005).

[7] Niigata City Historical Board, 85.

[8] Anonymous A, interview by author, April 13, 2005, notes. Even sixty years later, some residents of Niigata, Yokogōshi and Kyōgase would not speak about the events related to the downing of Jordan's B-29 unless they were promised anonymity. In these cases, each interviewee was given the designation, 'Anonymous A', 'Anonymous B', and so on. This follows a local precedent created by a Japanese research group who published a book on Niigata's POW history, entitled *Not Yet, that Bridge Between Us* (Kakehashi Imaharuka Editorial Committee. 架け橋、今遥か Not Yet, That Bridge Between Us. (Niigata City:

Kakehashi Imaharuka Editorial Committee,1999).). Several residents who contributed stories to that book also spoke only on the condition of anonymity.

[9] Kenneth Cambon, *Guest of Hirohito* (Vancouver: PW Press, 1990), 83. Doug Idlett, interview by author, March 25, 2004, MD Recording.

[10] John Duffy, 'Prisoner of War Camp 15-D, Niigata' (GHQ/SCAP Records, Record Group 331: Investigative Division Reports 18, NARA, Washington DC, 1947, photocopied).

[11] Niigata City Historical Board, 92.

[12] Frederick S. Hulse, 'Effects of War on Japanese Society,' *The Far Eastern Quarterly*, 7, no. 1 (November 1947), 32-33.

[13] United States Strategic Bombing Survey, *Summary Report (Pacific War)* (Washington, DC. Government Printing Office, 1946), 20-22, http://www.ibiblio.org/hyperwar/AAF/USSBS/PTO-Summary.html#thamotjc/ (accessed May 24, 2005).

[14] Frederick S. Hulse, 32.

[15] Diana Wright, 'Female Combatants and Japan's Meiji Restoration: The Case of Aizu,' *War in History*, 8, no. 4 (2001), 396-417.

[16] Diana Wright, 399. Bolitho, 266. There is some controversy as to whether Schnell was Dutch or German.

[17] Seiho Arima, 'The Western Influence on Japanese Military Science, Shipbuilding, and Navigation,' *Monumenta Nipponica*, 19, no. 3/4 (1964), 352-379.

[18] T.A. Bisson, 'The Zaibatsu's Wartime Role,' *Pacific Affairs*, 18, no. 4 (Dec., 1945), 355-368. Henry Graff, 'The Lesson of a Japanese Revolution,' *Political Science Quarterly*, 65, no.3 (Sep., 1950), 431-440. Kenneth Colegrove, 'Bases of Japan's East Asiatic Policies: Militarism in Japan's Foreign Policy,' *Annals of the American Academy of Political and Social Science*, 215, (May, 1941), 7-16.

[19] Nobuhide Sawamura, 'Local Spirit, Global Knowledge: a Japanese Approach to Knowledge Development in International Cooperation,' *Compare*, 32, no. 3 (2002), 339-348. Makoto Iokibe. 'Japan's Civil Society: A Historical Overview,' in Tadashi Yamamoto, (ed)., *Deciding the Public Good: Governance and Civil Society in Japan*. (Tokyo: Japan Center for International Exchange, 1999), http://www.jcie.or.jp/thinknet/pdfs/public_iokibe.pdf. (accessed November 13, 2006).

[20] W. Scott Morton & J. Kenneth Olenik, *Japan: Its History and Culture*. (New York: McGraw Hill, Inc., 2005), 162. Kenneth Colegrove, 7.

[21] Patrick Smith, *Japan: A Reinterpretation* (New York: Vintage Books, 1997), 58.

[22] Seiho Arima, 376-378. W. Scott Morton & J. Kenneth Olenik, 151.

[23] Peter Duus, 'Economic Dimensions of Meiji Imperialism: The Case of Korea,' in Ramon H. Myers and Mark R. Peattie (eds), *The Japanese Colonial Empire, 1895-1945* (Princeton: Princeton University Press, 1984), 132.

[24] Yoshio Ando, 'The Formation of Heavy Industry—One of the Processes of Industrialization in the Meiji Period,' *The Developing Economies*, 3, no. 4 (1965), 450-470.

[25] Isabella Bird, *Unbeaten Tracks in Japan (Reprint)*, (Whitefish, Montana: Kessinger Publishing 1878/2000), 86-89.

[26] Yoshio Ando, 469-470. Hiroshi Hazama, *The History of Labor Management in Japan*, (London: Macmillan Publishers, 1964/1997), 8.

[27] Kenneth Colegrove, 8. Winston Davis, *Japanese Religion and Society: Paradigms of Structure and Change*, (Albany, NY: State University Press of New York, 1992), 269-270. Junjiro Takakusu 'The Social and Ethical Value of the Family System in Japan,' *International Journal of Ethics*, 17, no. 1 (Oct., 1906), 100-106. Takakusu expresses a common line of thinking that continued until Japan's defeat: 'If the rulers are not fit rulers then the subjects are not obliged to accept them as rulers," and therefore if an emperor were incapable the people were relieved from obligations of loyalty; but in Japan there is nothing of the sort. No matter what character a ruler may have, we cling to him because he is

the representative of the Imperial line. He is the direct descendant of the father of the people. Thus Confucianism has been fundamentally modified since coming to Japan' (p. 104).

[28] Carol Gluck, *Japan's Modern Myths* (Princeton, New Jersey: Princeton University Press, 1985), 90.

[29] Karel van Wolferen, *The Enigma of Japanese Power* (New York: Alfred A. Knopf, 1989). Masaharu Anesaki, *History of Japanese Religion* (Tokyo: Charles E. Tuttle, 1963).

[30] Winston Davis, *Japanese Religion and Society: Paradigms of Structure and Change*, 218, 281.

[31] James Crowley, 'Japanese Army Factionalism in the Early 1930's,' *The Journal of Asian Studies*, 21, no. 3 (May, 1962), 309-326. Kenneth Kurihara, 'Japan's Educational System,' *Far Eastern Survey*, 13, no. 4 (Feb. 23, 1944), 35-38. Ben-Ami Shillony, 'Universities and Students in Wartime Japan,' *The Journal of Asian Studies*, 45, no. 4 (Aug., 1986), 769-787. Kenneth Colegrove, 13. Saburo Ienaga, 'The Glorification of War in Japanese Education,' *International Security*, 18, no.3 (Winter, 1993-1994), 113-133.

[32] Sarah Paine, *The Sino-Japanese War of 1894-1895: Perceptions, Power, and Primacy* (Cambridge: Cambridge University Press, 2003), 43-44.

[33] Sarah Paine, 152. Kozo Yamamura, 'Success Illgotten? The Role of Meiji Militarism in Japan's Technological Progress,' *The Journal of Economic History*, 37, no. 1 (Mar., 1977), 113-135.

[34] Alexis Wiren, 'The Lesson of Port Arthur,' *Russian Review*, 1, No. 2. (Apr., 1942), 40-43.

[35] Stanleigh Jones, 'Experiment and Tradition,' *Monumenta Nipponica*, 36, no. 2 (Summer, 1981), 115. William Nimmo, *Stars & Stripes Across the Pacific : The United States, Japan & the Asia/Pacific Region, 1895-1945* (Westport, Connecticut: Praeger Publishers, 2001), 65.

[36] Junjiro Takakusu, 100.

[37] Baron Kentaro Kaneko, 'Japan's Position in the Far East,' *Annals of the American Academy of Political and Social Science*, 26, (Jul., 1905), 80.

[38] William Nimmo, 64.

[39] Mochiji Rokusaburo (ed.), *Taiwan shokumin seisaku* (Taiwan Colonial Policy) (Tokyo: Fuzambo, 1912), 172-173, translated in Chang Han-Yu and Ramon Myers, 'Japanese Colonial Development Policy in Taiwan, 1895-1906: A Case of Bureaucratic Entrepreneurship,' *The Journal of Asian Studies*, 22, no. 4 (Aug., 1963), 436.

[40] W. Scott Morton & J. Kenneth Olenik, 169.

[41] Alvin Coox, 'Evidences of Antimilitarism in Prewar and Wartime Japan,' *Pacific Affairs*, 46, no. 4 (Winter 1973-1974), 502-514. Carlo Caldarola, 'Pacifism among Japanese Non-Church Christians,' *Journal of the American Academy of Religion*, 41, no. 4 (Dec., 1973), 506-519. W. Scott Morton & J. Kenneth Olenik, 171. W. Dean Kinzley, 'Japan in the World of Welfare Capitalism: Imperial Railroad Experiments with Welfare Work,' *Labor History*, 47, no. 2 (May 2006), 189–212.

[42] Akira Iriye, 'The Failure of Economic Expansionism: 1918-1931,' in *Japan in Crisis: Essays in Taisho Democracy*, Bernard S. Silberman and H. D. Harootunian (eds) (Princeton, N. J.: Princeton University Press, 1974), 245.

[43] 白川正雄 (Masao Shirakawa), interview by author, November 12, 2006, notes.

[44] David Mauk and John Oakland, *American Civilization: An Introduction* (London: Routledge, 2002), 56.

[45] W. Scott Morton & J. Kenneth Olenik, 172-177.

[46] Sannosuke Matsumoto, 'The Significance of Nationalism in Modern Japanese Thought: Some Theoretical Problems,' *The Journal of Asian Studies*, 31, no. 1 (Nov., 1971), 49-56.

[47] Kenneth Kurihara, 35-38. Ben-Ami Shillony, 769-787.

[48] Saburo Ienaga, 118-120. William Tsutsui, *Manufacturing Ideology: Scientific Management in Twentieth-Century Japan* (Princeton: Princeton University Press), 38-41. Kenneth Colegrove, 9.

[49] At least implicitly, the undertones of rural Japanese life may not have changed from those prewar days. Charles Jenkins, a former U.S. Army Sergeant who defected to North Korea during the Korean War, and who was allowed by the U.S. and Japan to live on Niigata Prefecture's Sado Island, a former penal colony and historic place of political exile, stated recently, 'After 40 years in North Korea, Japan is very easy to get adjusted to...I've had no problem whatsoever living here.' 'Jenkins finds the good life on Sado,' *The Japan Times Online*, February 1 2005, http://www.japantimes.co.jp/cgi-bin/getarticle.pl5?nn20050201f1.htm. (accessed January 4, 2006).

[50] Patrick Smith, 59.

[51] Haruko Taya Cook and Theodore F. Cook, *Japan at War: An Oral History* (New York: The New Press, 2000), 51.

[52] Ian Buruma, *Inventing Japan* (Westminster, MD, USA: Modern Library, 2003), 111.

[53] Haruko Taya Cook and Theodore F. Cook, 79.

[54] 佐藤俊司 (Shunji Sato), '一九四五年　七月二十日　京ヶ瀬村の一日（B29 焼山に落つ）July 20, 1945: A Day in Kyōgase Village (The B-29 Downing in Yakeyama),' 村誌 (*Village Historical Record*), 十一月 (November), 平成 14 年 (2002), 149.

[55] Alvin Coox, 513.

[56] Peter Wetzler, *Hirohito and War: Imperial Tradition and Military Decision Making in Pre-War Japan* (Honolulu: University of Hawaii Press, 1998), 13-14, 53-55.

[57] Hanama Tasaki, *Long the Imperial Way* (Boston: Houghton Miffin, 1950), 33.

[58] Frederick S. Hulse, 32.

[59] 稲垣真実 (Masumi Inagaki), 兵役を拒否した日本人 (*Japanese who Refused to Fight*) (Tokyo: Iwanami Shoten, 1972), 195.

[60] 白川正雄 (Masao Shirakawa), November 12, 2006.

[61] Niigata City Historical Board, 98.

[62] 網干嘉一郎 (Kiichiro Amihoshi) '戦時中の記録 (War Memories),' (郷土新潟 (*Hometown Niigata*) 6 (February, 1965)), 16.

[63] 小松重男 (Shigeo Komatsu) 幕末遠国奉行の日記 (*Diary of an Administrator at the Close of Edo's Military Rule*) (Tokyo: (中央松論社) Chuo Matsuron, 1989). アーネスト・サトウ (Sir Ernest Mason Satow)一外交官の見た明示維新 （下）(*A Diplomat in Japan*) (Tokyo: 岩波書店 (Iwanami Shoten), 1960/1994), 9-12. That Britain had its eye on Niigata is certain. Dr. William Willis, who had been sent to give medical aid to Imperial troops during the Japanese Civil War (the *Bōshin Sensō*), took copious notes about Niigata's potential as a port for the silk trade. He was particularly interested in its capacity to support medium-sized ships, and of its good local administration. As cited in Gordon Daniels, 'The Japanese Civil War (1868) -- A British View,' *Modern Asian Studies*, 1, no 3 (1967), 245-246, 261.

[64] Robert Grant, interview by author, April 23, 2004, MD Recording.

[65] T. H. Moorer (Interrogator), 'Interrogation Nav. No. 5 USSBS No. 34 Allied Offensive Mining Campaign (Interrogation of: Captain TAMURA, Kyuzo, IJN. War Time Duties were Devoted to Mine Construction and Mine Sweeping),' in *United States Strategic Bombing Survey (Pacific)*, ed. Naval Analysis Division (Washington, DC.: Naval Analysis Division, 1945), 20, http://www.ibiblio.org/hyperwar/AAF/USSBS/IJO/IJO-5.html. (accessed September 21, 2005).

[66] '投下訓練兼ね飛来 (For Bombing and Training They Came),' 新潟日報 (*Niigata Nippo*), August 12 1992, sec. 社会 (Society), 22.

[67] 20th Air Force Headquarters, *Tactical Mission Report (9/10 July to 14/15 August)*, 116. 20th Air Force, *Air Intelligence Report* (San Francisco: Commanding General, USASTAF, APO 234, 1945), 20-22.

[68] 網干嘉一郎 (Kiichiro Amihoshi), 15.

PART TWO

THE LAST MISSION

CHAPTER FIVE

ENDGAME

Despite Burkle's dire prediction, the Jordan Crew's missions during the previous month had been successful. Many of their missions had been to drop mines in the Shimonoseki Straits. Wride's injuries were mending. The new plane had been reliable. After early difficulties that resulting in at least one failed mission, Trump's targeting skills had improved dramatically – so much in fact that after one mission, the crew was awarded with a case of cold beer from Col. Gibson. Trump had found his place on the crew. He and Burkle had discovered their common Christian devotion and had become friends. The crew had only three missions to go and it looked like the worst was behind them. Hopes soared when word came that everyone would be home by the middle of August.[1]

Jordan Crew over the Shimonoseki Straits
(W.M. Rice, ed., *Pirate's Log: A Historical Record of the Sixth Bombardment Group*,
Manila: 2771st Engr. Base Reproduction Co, 1946, 20.)

Kruvant's mental health, however, had steadily grown worse. During the past few missions, his anxiety attacks had become so severe that he was barely able to perform his duties. The central fire controller's position was vital for guiding the other gunners in point defense and Jordan was worried that Kruvant had become a danger to both himself and the rest of the crew. He had learned that Kruvant's brother had been killed in the D-Day invasion at Normandy. This made Kruvant the last surviving son in his family. Upon Garin's advice Jordan kept this news a secret. Both feared that the shock might push him over the edge. When Garin arrived back in New York, he immediately contacted Kruvant's family about putting in a request for their son's return to the US. Garin was relieved to be able to keep his promise to help take care of Kruvant, but he worried for the rest of his crew. Would their luck hold out?

Fateful Decisions

On July 18, the Jordan Crew was resting from a mining mission the night before to the port of Rashin, Korea. Most of the Imperial Japanese ports along the Japan Sea coast had minimal anti-aircraft crews and virtually no fighter support. Although the mission to Rashin had been easy, it had also been the longest of the entire war, totaling over twenty-one hours, including the time the crew had to stop at Iwo Jima to refuel. As the navigator, Trump had stayed awake during the entire mission to give navigation readings to the pilot or copilot. The rest of the crew had slept in shifts. When Jordan got the call for another mining mission to the port city of Niigata, he said it would be up to Trump to decide whether or not they would take this mission. Jordan sent the gunners over to Trump's hut to find out what he wanted to do.[2]

Trump was fast asleep in his bunk when the gunners came. They eagerly assured him that the mission to Niigata would be another milk run. Trump blearily looked at their haggard, expectant faces. This mission would put them one step closer to finishing their tour of duty. He told them to get ready to go.[3]

The ground crews were loading magnetic mines into the plane and the crew was going through preflight checks when suddenly the military police came. They promptly escorted a confused Kruvant to another part of the base. His parents' request had been granted just in time. A replacement crewman by the name of Walter Dickerson was brought in at the last moment to be the central fire controller. Dickerson had been in the military longer than even Jordan, though all of his postings had been stateside. This was the first mission of his first tour of duty.

The Mission

The mission briefing for Niigata was straightforward. Five planes from the 6th Bombardment Group would leave early in the evening of July 19 and head towards Japan via Iwo Jima.

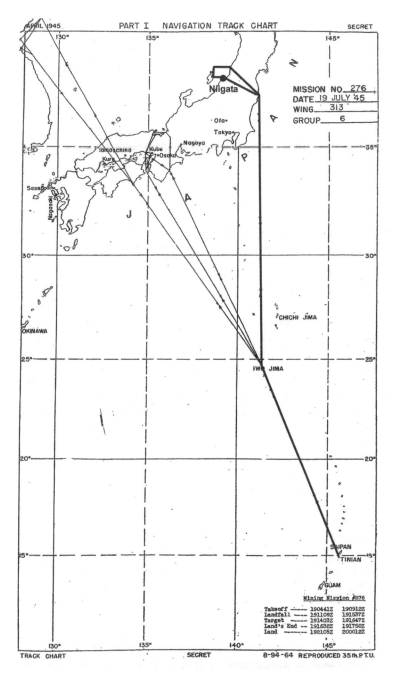

The Jordan Crew's Route to Niigata.
(Tactical Mission Reports July 9/10 to August 14/15. San Francisco: Commanding General, USASTAF, APO 234, 1945, 21.)

After nearing the coast near Sendai, they would fly west over the mountains, circle the straits between Sado Island and Niigata, and make their approach on Minefield UNCLE. Each crew would come in one at a time, drop an assortment of naval mines, follow the Agano River back towards the Alps and return via the same route back to Tinian.

The flight from Tinian to the Japanese coast near Sendai was long, dull and uneventful. Some of the crewmen slept in the rest bunks of the rear cabin. Trump struggled to stay alert as he looked at his instrument panels, which provided the only illumination in the dark cabin. Nobody spoke.

The B-29s approached Sendai at around 12:00 AM on July 20. They were soon detected by a Japanese observation post. A radio announcement was broadcast that B-29s had been spotted, and that their anticipated destination was Niigata.[4] Another listening post later verified that the planes were approaching Niigata, and sometime before 1:00 am, air raid sirens sounded throughout the city. People scrambled to put out the lights and slipped on homemade padded clothing that offered some protection from falling flak shrapnel and sparks.[5] One early unpublished account of that night describes the first moments of apprehension in the city.

> In the city of Niigata itself the people hurried to bomb shelters. Kensaku Omi, a medical student with a hard Prussian face, was carrying two small dolls to his foster mother. He stumbled in the dark, fell and broke the arm of one. Fumiko, a maid in the Niigata Hotel, too excited to remember her getas, ran out barefooted. Sanjerau, the tiny bus driver, pulled his immaculate vehicle to the side of the road and being of gentle nature calmly waited. Jakob Fischer, a German expatriate, ran from his house to the top of a sand dune. Below him the sea which growled over from Vladivostok broke in foam on the beach.[6]

Allied POWs at Niigata Camps 5B and 15B also went outside their hovels to watch as the searchlights began 'moving across the sky…like shiny swords against a background of black velvet.'[7]

There is a haunting sound that a B-29 makes as it approaches. It is described by those who heard it as something between a low howl and a deep rumble.[8] Residents peered into the night sky and listened as, from over the harbor, that familiar, awful sound began to swell from unseen engines.

Flying in the Shadows

As the lead plane, Jordan made the first run. They came in low to about 600 meters over the bay. Wride announced the opening of the bomb bay doors. Adams began giving radar readings to Trump, who navigated their route and recorded the position of the mines on a template overlay as each parachuted to the murky waters below. A few perfunctory flak bursts began to pop here and there, but none were close enough to cause alarm. After all, every other crew that had mined Niigata's harbor had returned unscathed and the Jordan Crew was still cloaked in darkness. Everyone was focused on their tasks. When the last mine was away, Wride closed the bomb bay doors and Jordan began the languid climb that would take them home.

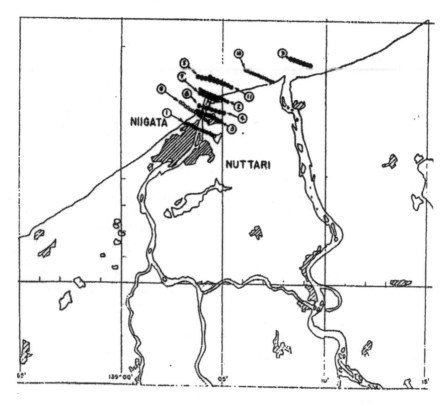

Navigator's Plot of Mining Missions over Minefield UNCLE (Niigata) on July 19/20 and 28. Plots 1 -5 are from July 19/20. The remaining plots are from a mission on July 28. Jordan's plane was #1. These plots, extrapolated from debriefings of other crews that returned to Tinian, indicate that most of the mines dropped by the Jordan Crew that night fell on Niigata City, but Jordan's surviving crewmen strongly contend that all of their mines landed in the harbor, not on the city.
(Tactical Mission Reports July 9/10 to August 14/15 Navigation Maps. San Francisco: Commanding General, USASTAF, APO 234, 1945, 24.)

It was at this moment that the Jordan Crew made a fateful decision. Instead of giving the readings which, according to the mission briefing, would have taken them in an easterly direction away from Niigata City, Trump gave Jordan the direct heading for returning home, This took them in a southerly direction over the center of Niigata City. No one was aware that this also put them directly over a dozen anti-aircraft emplacements just in from Tokyo, all of which were armed with radar controlled searchlights.

Years later Trump wrote, 'At twenty-one, I guess I was a little cocky, however, going direct often saved an hour or even two.'[9] Deviating from the flight plan and returning direct was always permissible during a crew emergency. However, returning in order to cut a couple of hours off of one's flight time was equally a temptation for war weary air crews. This time especially, since both Trump and the rest of the Jordan Crew were exhausted from their earlier mission to Rashin. None relished facing another seven hours back to Tinian in cramped conditions. Trump also mentioned that they had returned direct on a number of earlier missions, which suggests that Jordan, as the ranking officer, was either aware or should have been aware of what was going on. Regardless of who knew what, at the moment, the point was moot. This was the wrong night for taking a short cut home. The Jordan Crew had just started to relax when suddenly and unexpectedly, they found themselves blinking in the glare of a searchlight.

Niigata residents had watched the searchlights drifting lazily to and fro, and then as one suddenly whipped across the sky to lock on to Jordan's B-29. Many gasped first in shock at the unexpected speed of the searchlight, and then again as they felt overwhelming waves of horror, hatred, awe and defeat at seeing Jordan's sleek behemoth rumbling overhead. Their first impressions were something akin to, 'How can we win against that?'[10]

More searchlights rapidly began to tighten their grip on the Jordan Crew. Volleys of anti-aircraft fire started to burst around them with new vigor. Slowly, a red targeting spotlight drifted upwards and rested on the center of the plane. The onlookers below held their breath, waiting to see what would happen. In a few more seconds the B-29 would be too far away for a clear shot.[11]

The crewmen onboard were also holding their breath. With the exception of Trump and Dickerson, everyone remembered what happened the last time they had been caught in the searchlights on that terrifying mission over Tokyo. Like then, darkness had been their friend. At this low altitude, in their huge and sluggish B-29, they were again in extreme danger. All the Jordan Crew could do now was to try and run the gauntlet of flak. Air crews from the other B-29s who had finished their runs could only look on helplessly at what was to happen next.[12]

A shudder went through the entire plane. The crew looked out to confirm their worst fears. The inner nacelle of their left wing was smoking. They had been hit.

Trading Places

On the ground, the inhabitants of Niigata and the surrounding villages saw the flak hit its mark with a crack and a flash. There was a split second of disbelief, followed by shouts of, 'Oh, look! It's been hit! It's burning! It's going down!'[13] Across the entire area people erupted into shouts of unrestrained delight, as if they were watching a summer fireworks display.[14] Shunkichi Shimizu, a reporter for the *Niigata Nippo*, the local newspaper, remembers the moment vividly.

When the top of the plane burst into flame in the darkness I clapped my hands in joy. People around me shouted, 'Banzai! Banzai!' A woman in the bus said she had been so glad to see the plane dive to the earth that she laid her baby on the ground beside her and clapped her hands. Such was the emotion of the people.[15]

Grainy photo from the front page of the *Niigata Nippo* on July 21, 1945. The white streak in the upper right corner is Jordan's plane as it burned in the nighttime sky. The ghostly figures at the bottom are Niigata citizens in clothing designed to offer protection from flak.

War stories are replete with tragic twists of fate. The tale of that early morning on July 20 is no exception. At the moment Jordan's plane began to burn in the sky, an extraordinary transaction took place. What before had been for the citizens of Niigata an unassailable icon of death now had become a blazing symbol of hope. For the Jordan Crew, however, what had only moments before been for them a stronghold of American superiority now was rapidly becoming a brittle, burning deathtrap.

A Village Fete

On the outskirts of Niigata, along the Agano River, in a small hamlet on the far side of the village of Yokogōshi known as Yakeyama (which in Japanese means, 'Scorch Mountain'), a group of villagers were huddled together and shouting 'banzai'. One wit by the name of Kuwabara began to chant *'kuwabara, kuwabara, kuwabara'*, which as a Japanese pun, also sounds like the words of an incantation used to chase away demons. People laughed at the irony as the American demons above were being exorcised from their skies.[16] Very quickly, however, this impromptu party fell still as, one by one, they looked upward toward the sky with gaping stares of horror. The burning B-29 was headed straight towards them.[17]

Fire in the Sky

Jordan opened the engines up to full throttle as Wride shouted over the intercom, 'I'm gonna get those lights!' He took control of the forward guns and started shooting at the searchlights below. One searchlight went out. 'I got one!'[18] Down below in the hamlet called Kawaneyauchi, the bullets rained down on the tile roofs of several homes. One bullet penetrated the roof of one house and shattered a kitchen cupboard inside.[19]

Trump now gave Jordan the navigation readings that would take them back along the Agano River and towards the mountains. Jordan followed the readings and raced to escape the anti-aircraft batteries. He tried feathering the damaged propeller but it kept spinning. Apparently flak had cut the oil lines and power to the controls. A friction-induced fire was beginning to flicker. It grew brighter. Any moment and the fuel lines in their left wing could catch fire. McGraw anticipated that the fire might spread to both wings through the fuel lines and from his control station cut off the fuel supply to the port inner engine and feathered its propeller.[20] The fire ignored them.

Jordan put the plane into a series of sharp dives in an attempt to blow out the flames. After the third dive, the fire went out. The crew could not believe their luck. They breathed a collective sigh of relief.

It was too soon to feel fortunate. The flames flashed up again, this time with even greater ferocity, and spread to the belly of the plane. In the aft cabin Grant watched as the fire now began to melt the Perspex dome of his gun-aiming position. 'How is everything back there?' called Jordan on the intercom. 'We're OK,' said Grant, 'what's happening up there?' 'We've been hit,' said Jordan, and then through garbled static, a furtive, '…it's bad.'

The flames were now trailing so far behind the plane that it looked like a meteor streaking across the sky. Other B-29 crews could see Jordan's plane burning brightly in the distance.[21] Some described it as like an orange flare trailing across the night sky.[22] Even Spero could see the flames from his vantage point in the rear turret. 'What the hell's going on up there?' he called over the intercom.

'We've been hit!' shouted Grant.

70

Grant tossed down his interphone to get out of the turret. The smoke and heat had quickly become unbearable. Dickerson continued to inform the front cabin about the growing flames from the Central Fire Control position.

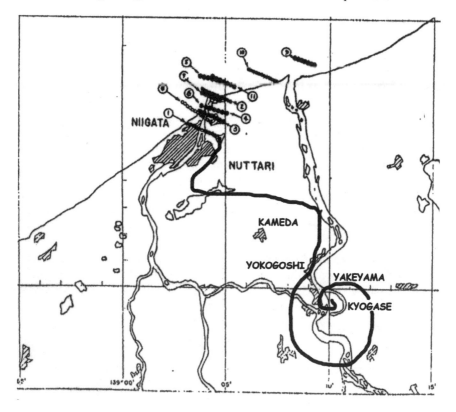

Flight path of Jordan's plane as it went down outside the hamlet of Yakeyama, a ward of Yokogōshi Village.
(Tactical Mission Reports, Navigation Maps, 24 and Yokogōshi Village History, 745.)

In the front of the plane, Hawkins was staring forward, transfixed, while Jordan considered what to do. McGraw was still struggling to find some way to cut off the fuel supply to the left wing. Nothing seemed to work. Thick, toxic smoke began to fill the cabin. Oil pressure was dropping fast. 'Let's get the hell out of here! Prepare to jump!' barked Jordan over the intercom. He turned on the cabin lights, which were virtually useless in the smoke-filled cabin. 'Bomb bay doors coming open,' shouted Wride from the nose of the plane. The doors groaned open once more. Jordan turned on the exterior navigation lights and rang the alarm bell, signaling that now was the time to bail out.

'Hitting Silk'

In the front cabin, Trump was not wearing his bulky parachute. Like Garin, he had been confident that he would never be shot down. He had always put his parachute in the corner of his cramped navigator's station. Now he scrambled to put it on as he watched McGraw and Wiernik bail out through the bomb bay. Jordan stood up and turned to leave. Hawkins remained in his seat, staring forward. 'Let's go,' shouted Jordan over the drone of the engines. Hawkins didn't seem to hear him. Jordan ripped off Hawkins' helmet. 'Come on!' Hawkins stood up, and as if he were sleepwalking, started to follow Jordan, who had just bailed out.[23] Trump was watching this scene as he fastened his parachute buckles, and couldn't believe his eyes when he saw Hawkins calmly turn around and walk back to the copilot's seat. Trump was now ready to jump. But first he went to Hawkins and shook him, shouting, 'Let's go!' Hawkins didn't pay any attention. Wride had now popped up from the bombardier's station. Wride and Hawkins looked intensely at each other, talking quietly. Trump was taken aback. The situation was becoming progressively surreal. Flames were now beginning to roll up inside the cabin from the forward bomb bay doors. He turned and bailed out through the flames head first, not knowing if either man had followed him.[24]

After the bomb bay doors had been reopened the gunners in the rear of the plane had been scrambling back and forth in preparation for the inevitable. One of the gunners, most likely Burkle, assumed that they had been spotted by a radar-guided searchlight and had been 'dispensing rope' to jam any radar that might still be tracking them. Adams went over and told him that they were preparing to bail out, and then ran back to his small radar cubicle to put on his parachute.[25]

The alarm sounded. Dickerson bailed out. Grant banged on Adam's door, 'You coming?' he shouted.

'Yeah, just a second,' came the muffled reply.

Grant made his way towards the bomb bay doors. Burkle was there looking down, frozen, and blocking the exit. 'Let's get the hell out of here!' yelled Grant as he gave Burkle a ferocious shove. Burkle disappeared like a puff of smoke in the night. This moment tortured Grant for the rest of the evening: Had he just killed his friend, or did Burkle make it?

He looked over his shoulder. Spero had crawled up from the rear turret into their cabin shouting to Adams, 'I'm going!'

'I'm right behind you!' came Adams' voice from the gloom.

Grant bailed out at that moment. He pulled his ripcord and looked to the left to see the plane, now almost entirely engulfed in flames, as it began to circle slowly and then suddenly drop. Seconds later, he heard the awful crash.[26]

---

[1] Florio Spero, June 26, 1945, war diary, Spero Family Collection, Homer Glen, Illinois.
[2] Paul Trump, 'War Memories,' 2003, unpublished manuscript (photocopy), 2. Trump Family Papers, Lititz, PA.
[3] Paul Trump, 'War Memories,' 2.

[4] 佐藤俊司 (Shunji Sato), '一九四五年　七月二十日　京ヶ瀬村の一日（B29 焼山に落つ）July 20, 1945: A Day in Kyōgase Village (The B-29 Downing in Yakeyama),' 村誌 (Village Historical Record), 十一月 (November), 平成 14 年 (2002), 149.

[5] Anonymous A, interview by author, April 13, 2005, notes.

[6] Valery Burati, 'Fragments of a Mission,' 1972, unpublished manuscript (typewritten), 1, George McGraw Private Papers, Gillett, Arkansas.

[7] William Howard Chittenden, *From China Marine to Jap POW* (Paducah, Kentucky: Turner Publishing Company, 1995), 167.

[8] Takurou Munezawa, interview by author, October 15, 2003, notes.

[9] Paul Trump, Lititz, PA, to Hitoshi Fukuda, Questionnaires to B-29 Crewmen Lost over Yokogoshi, Yokogoshi Town Department of History, Yokogoshi, Niigata, Japan.

[10] Nobu Yoshioka, interview by author, October 3, 2003, notes. Yoshihiro Honda, interview by author, May 2, 2005, notes. Anonymous A, April 13, 2005. Chozo Shimizu, Kyomi Shimizu, Choei Nagai, Miyo Meguro, Masao Saito, Rinbei Kuga, interview by Toshihide Uemura, July 1, 1998, tape recording.

[11] Anonymous A, April 13, 2005.

[12] Robert K. Hall, 'Report on Capt. (Now Major) Gordon P. Jordan and Crew, Missing in Action 19/20 July 1945' (San Francisco, California: Sixth Bombardment Group, Office of the Group Intelligence Officer, 15 August, 1945, photocopied), 1-2.

[13] Anonymous A, April 13, 2005.

[14] Chozo Shimizu, Kyomi Shimizu, Choei Nagai, Miyo Meguro, Masao Saito, Rinbei Kuga, July 1, 1998.

[15] Valery Burati, 2.

[16] 金塚友之丞 (Tomoyuki Kanazuka), '横越村焼山へ落ちた B29 と京ヶ瀬村へ降りた落下傘 (The B-29 that went down in Yokogoshi and Those who parachuted into Kyōgase),' 郷土新潟 (Hometown Niigata) 6 (February 1965), 9.

[17] 植村敏秀 (Toshihide Uemura), '暁部隊　(The Akatsuki Regiment),' 新潟市合併町村の歴史研究報告 (Niigata Municipal Town and Village Incorporation Historical Research Bulletin 4 (March 1984), 44-45.

[18] Edmund Steffler (Capt.), 'Missing Air Crew Report #14786' (College Park, Maryland: NARA, 1945, July 23, photocopied).

[19] Yoshikazu Nakamura, interview by Toshihide Uemura, July 1, 1998, tape recording, The B-29 Downing Incident (B29 撃墜事件について), Former Yokogōshi City History Department, Yokogōshi, Niigata.

[20] Paul Trump, interview by author, March 23, 2004, MD Recording.

[21] Edmund Steffler (Capt.), 'Missing Air Crew Report #14786'.

[22] Robert K. Hall, 1-2.

[23] Edmund Steffler (Capt.), 'Missing Air Crew Report #14786'.

[24] Paul Trump, interview by author, September 13, 2004, MD Recording. Paul Trump, March 23, 2004.

[25] Edmund Steffler (Capt.), 'Missing Air Crew Report #14786'.

[26] Robert Grant, interview by author, April 23, 2004, MD Recording.

CHAPTER SIX

VILLAGES ON THE FRINGE

Tadashi Saito took a long drag on his cigarette, 'When we were kids, we were worse off than the bums living over at Niigata Station.'[1] His two friends nodded in silent agreement.

I was sitting on a Japanese straw mat floor. A cup of green tea had been offered with simple elegance. A kerosene space heater was close by. On top of it, an old teakettle bubbled and squeaked. The room was quiet, almost heavy, as I patiently waited for the three old men to study me with silent suspicion. These were some of the villagers of Yakeyama who saw Jordan's B-29 go down near their homes, and who had witnessed much of what followed. The crash site was only about 250 meters from the small traditional house in which we were sitting. Outside, a light snow was falling.

Village Life

The former villages of Yakeyama, Yokogōshi and Kyōgase were only about fifteen kilometers from Niigata. But the unpaved road conditions in the 1940s created the feeling that these villages were much farther away. Culturally and socially, village life was far removed from the hard-nosed bustle of Niigata City. In many ways the area where the Jordan Crew landed that night had much in common with the rural farming towns of their own childhood. Each town had its own collection of wise elders, village fools, local heroes, bullies, and hard-working pillars of society. On any given day, they could be earthy, friendly, kind or wary. An outsider was typically anyone whose family had not lived in the area for more than three generations. As in many rural communities around the world, those living on the outskirts of Niigata followed unspoken codes of conduct that conformed to long-established roles. During wartime these attitudes and practices had become warped by the absurd jumble of religion, racism and nationalism in support for a government that barely acknowledged their existence. They were, as they are anywhere, simple country folk.

With the exception of a few, such as Keiichi Meguro, the Village Ward, most in Yakeyama were tenant farmers of the local land baron, Bunkichi Itō. Their memory of those days was one of a life lived in harmony with the cycle of the seasons. Depending on the weather they either stayed inside to do what was necessary to prepare for the upcoming season, or worked outside in the fields, tilling the soil and harvesting crops for the war effort. Most of the food they produced went to the government, but they still found ways to keep a little for themselves. Although it was against the law, they would fish the nearby Agano River or catch the occasional rabbit that was foolish enough to stray near the village. Compared to people in Niigata, they ate better, but from their point-of-view, they still didn't have enough.[2]

Rice being collected from near Yakeyama for the war effort.
(Photo courtesy of Hitoshi Fukuda.)

The memories of people from other sections of Japanese society about their country cousins are quite different. As the war dragged on, the system of rationing had virtually collapsed partly because the farmers were hoarding food. Trains were often packed with city dwellers making trips to the country to get care packages from their relatives. Although this practice was strictly illegal, the local police usually worked out an arrangement where they would look the other way so long as such visits did not become too noticeable or too frequent. People who lacked personal connections had to buy food at exorbitant prices on the black market. Those who didn't have money didn't eat.[3]

To deal with the food shortage, the Japanese government changed the system of rental payments for tenant farmers. Instead of the traditional payments of rice or produce to the land barons, they were allowed to pay in cash. All food was to go to the war effort. This was disastrous for land barons. Rice was worth far more than money – and far more edible. The power and status of land barons continued to decline, while that of the farmers, who were making a considerable amount of money on the black market, continued to rise.

After the war, the transfer of power was made complete when the Occupation Government broke up the land barons' property and redistributed it to the farmers. In the summer of 1945, farmers were already rising to the top of the society because of their access to food. Socially, however, they were detested by city dwellers, who saw them as greedy, grubbing, boorish peasants who were remorselessly profiting off the misfortunes caused by the war.[4]

Yokogōshi women's local defense brigade on review in early 1945.
(Photo courtesy of Hitoshi Fukuda.)

Yokogōshi's War

Except for older veterans, most people living in the villages were women and children. Younger men and teenaged boys were immediately drafted and expected to do their part to protect Japan. As the war progressed, and as surrounded Japanese units were exhorted to fight to the last man, these tours of duty turned into a deadly lottery. Residents remember that over five-hundred students from one graduating class of a school near Kyōgase had been sent to the South Pacific in early 1944. By 1945, all were reported as either killed or missing in action.[5]

Turmoil simmered in the hearts of women who had to care for the children, elderly family members and other relatives who had fled the bombed-out cities. There was considerable friction between family members as time went on. Their husbands and sons were doing their part for the greater good of the family of Japan, but the daily struggle to keep those still at home fed, combined with the thought that their husbands and sons might never return was a heavy burden that most of the womenfolk carried in silence. Publicly, such a death was regarded as an honor, as Junjiro Takakusu explains.

A parent whose child is killed, although at first he may be inclined to rush to help, yet will grit his teeth and say like Masaoka: 'It is for the sake of our lord and master.' When a telegram comes from army headquarters telling of the death of a husband on the battlefield, it is this spirit that makes wives rejoice that their husbands have fulfilled a soldier's duty. In the West when a man dies, his wife upon hearing of it is likely to faint away, but in Japan a wife curbs the natural emotions under the impulse to see that the family does not suffer.[6]

So went the official line, which left women with little in the way of an acceptable outlet for their natural human emotions. To express grief for too long would be a disgrace. An American counterpart to such sentiment still exists today in rural fundamentalist Christian circles, where some would secretly look down upon the brother or sister grieving too long over the loss of a loved one. Unless there is an expression of joy for their passing into Heaven, such grief suggests weak convictions and a tenuous place in the community of faith. The women of the villages outside of Niigata stoically maintained their public face of faithful obedience to the Emperor, and when required, sacrificed their sons and husbands to further the family of Japan. But in their huts late at night, many would collapse under the weight of their private depression, until it was punctuated by the frustration of the next morning.

In the years leading up to the war, villagers rarely finished elementary school. During the war, students of all ages spent less time studying and more time on work details for the war effort. By 1945, except for research institutes, schools had been closed by the government in order to mobilize all but the youngest of children to work as laborers for the war effort and to prepare for the decisive final battle for the home islands (*hondo kessen*).[7] In Yokogōshi, the young boys and girls spent their days collecting scraps for recycling, loading crates on trucks, or working in someone else's field. Beatings for the slightest infraction were a regular occurrence.[8] Boys were taught to fight with bamboo spears in the same way that women were trained for the local defense brigades. Hulse discovered that the plan to train women and children as a resistance force against the American invasion had actually been implemented by bureaucrats from the peace factions of the government. In the indirect manner of communication that is common in the upper echelons of Japanese society, the intended message was that the war would soon be over. They were surprised when their indirectness was lost upon many women and children in the countryside, who often demonstrated that they would be willing to bravely defend their country for the Emperor.[9] While some rose to the task with the zeal of a new recruit who has never seen war, others carried thoughts of avenging their family members before joining them in death.

Very few questioned the regular abuse and mounting burdens. They had rarely experienced anything else. This was the way of things in their dirty, daily grind. With the exception of the required marches for the local brigade, the latest rumor about another local boy being killed abroad, or stories of ships sinking somewhere near Niigata, the war for many in tiny wards like Yakeyama still seemed like an abstraction far removed from their daily trouble.[10] That quickly changed as the blazing hulk of Jordan's B-29 grew ever larger as it hurtled towards their homes.

The Final Descent

They watched the plane come up the Agano River and circle back sharply over the vicinity of Kyōgase Village. It looked to them as if the pilot was slowly descending in a search for a place to land.[11] They saw an engine fall off and burn brightly as it tumbled to the ground. Observers in Niigata also saw the light of this burning engine, and many believed that a second B-29 had been downed, because there are many who state they saw two planes hit that evening.[12]

Eyewitness sketch of Jordan's B-29 as it approached Yokogōshi and Kyōgase. (Shunji Sato, 'July 20, 1945: A Day in Kyōgase Village (The B-29 Downing in Yakeyama),' *Village Historical Record*, (November, 2002), 150.)

Rumors spread later among the villagers about a second B-29 that had crashed in the mountains somewhere in Fukushima Prefecture. Harry George, who flew as a copilot on another B-29 during the same mining mission over Niigata that night, confirmed that all the other crews returned.[13] An intelligence report which debriefed returning crews states that several had been hit by very accurate and heavy flak that was guided by at least 15 radar controlled searchlights.[14] Trump mentioned once that just before he jumped, he looked out the window and thought he saw another plane that was burning, but given the conditions he couldn't be certain.[15] There is an additional account from a Robert Gertenbach of the 9th Bombardment Group, who mentions the terror he felt when his plane had an engine fire on a night mining mission over Niigata.[16] These accounts tend to lend credence to the memories of those on the ground that at least another plane was burning in the air for a brief period of time, since no other B-29s were ever observed to be hit over Niigata on any other evenings.[17]

Jordan's plane approached Yakeyama. Burning fragments showered the village as the plane passed overhead. One large piece of flaming metal slammed into the roof of Kuwabara's hut, causing considerable damage.[18] The plane looped around again, descending as if it were going to land on Yakeyama itself.

A few hundred meters in the air the left wing snapped off. The B-29 began to twirl like a maple seed in autumn as it spewed fire, smoke and wreckage in all directions. The ground shook with the force of an earthquake as the flaming craft smashed into a nearby field of sweet potatoes.[19]

There was a moment of stunned silence. The plane was no longer burning. All was dark. Then tiny flames started to lick the sides of the B-29 once more, and the fire quickly became large and bright enough for everyone to see each other's face clearly. Two more B-29s flew overhead, piloted by Capt. Jacob Schad and Lt. William Meadows, who had witnessed the event from the air. Schad's heart broke as he saw the fire blazing below. He and Jordan had become very close friends during those nights of bourbon and gambling. He veered away from Yokōgoshi and back towards Tinian. The fire soon dwindled to a twinkle. His crew noticed that Schad's youthful zeal faded following that night.[20]

Someone in the village cried out in fright and pointed to the sky: Several parachutes were slowly descending towards the rice paddies about a kilometer away near Kyōgase.[21] Even from Niigata City, many people, including Allied POWs, could see the parachutes of crewmen escaping the plane.[22] A radio in a nearby window had been left on, and everyone heard a bulletin now warning that an undetermined number of enemy soldiers had been sighted parachuting just outside of Niigata. They were to be considered armed and dangerous. People began to feel increasingly frightened, and they muttered to each other about what to do.

Suddenly, hundreds of gunshots pierced the night. Bullets were flying everywhere, hitting houses and whizzing past the villagers' heads. Panic-stricken, everyone scattered in all directions, screaming.[23]

A Terrible Misunderstanding

The fire that was consuming the B-29 had reached the machine gun ammunition stores in the front cabin. The villagers' fear turned into a fierce protective anger as they thought that the Americans were shooting at them from across the field. Their homes and families were under attack.[24]

When the shots had died down, the men told the women to stay inside while they ventured out with a few of the older boys. There was one man in the village that had a rifle, but he was too afraid to lead the group. He followed in the rear while others took bamboo spears and crept up to the crash site.[25] The nose of the B-29 was partially buried in the muddy field. The tail section was slightly elevated in the air. Most of the plane was engulfed in flames.

Soon word came across the fields from the civil defense units (keibō-dan) that all available men had been ordered to track down and capture the Americans. A hodgepodge of retired soldiers, firefighters, farmers, air raid wardens, schoolboys and a few wives gathered into groups.[26] Some had swords and firearms, but most carried clubs, bamboo spears or a Japanese implement used for controlling fires known as a tobikuchi. When sharpened, it could become a deadly weapon.

Eyewitness sketch of Jordan's B-29 soon after impact.
(Shunji Sato, 'July 20, 1945: A Day in Kyōgase Village (The B-29 Downing in Yakeyama),' *Village Historical Record*, (November, 2002), 150.)

Racing against Time

National guardsmen and soldiers from the local POW camps in Niigata were also mobilizing as fast as they could to capture the B-29 crewmen. But getting to the crash site was taking time: The fire could be seen from far away and throngs of people from the surrounding villages had clogged the roads in a rush to see the action. Passengers also overloaded a ferry crossing the river to Yakeyama, and an undetermined number of people drowned in the Agano River.[27] Others who had not been lost in the river were stretched out on both shores in need of medical assistance.[28] In the race between professional soldiers and local villagers to find the Jordan Crew, the villagers in Kyōgase and Yakeyama had a significant head start.

Most of the crew's parachutes were spotted landing close to Kyōgase Village. Sixty years ago, a meander in the Agano River almost completely separated Yokogōshi from Kyōgase. Men from Yokogōshi ran in the direction of the parachutes, but the residents in the Kyōgase area were the first to make contact with members of the Jordan Crew.[29]

The manhunt was on. Bands of villagers stalked the narrow roads that crisscrossed their rice paddies, barns, culverts and fields. Some had hand-cranked flashlights, but most crept quietly in the dark. The rustle of rice stalks or the quiet plop in a distant paddy on any other night would have been the peaceful sounds of a summer evening. This night, however, every noise set them on edge: Somewhere out there, hiding in the dark, were armed enemy soldiers. Something primal began to take over.

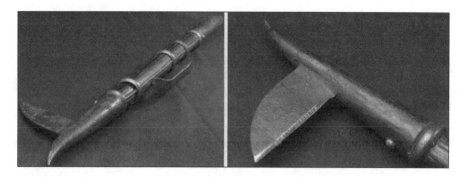

Japanese *tobikuchi*. Many villagers used this instrument to attack and capture members of the Jordan Crew.

They clutched their spears with sweaty hands as they hunted the American demons. There was a feeling of oneness with the national cause. There was no thought of right or wrong. They were as focused as deer hunters stalking their prey. Some of the older boys saw this as their chance to fulfill promises given to their fathers to protect their families. It was now their opportunity to gain glory in same way as their elder brothers had found it fighting abroad.[30] Before the night was out, this lethal mix of motivations and emotions would result in tragic consequences for members of the Jordan Crew.

---

[1] Motoichi Fujita, Tadashi Saito, Hikaru Sato, interview by author, January 16, 2004, MD Recording.

[2] Motoichi Fujita, Tadashi Saito, Hikaru Sato, January 16, 2004.

[3] Frederick S. Hulse, 'Effects of War on Japanese Society,' *The Far Eastern Quarterly* 7, no. 1 (November 1947), 28.

[4] Frederick S. Hulse, 29-31.

[5] Anonymous B, interview by author, June 20, 2003, notes.

[6] Junjiro Takakusu, 'The Social and Ethical Value of the Family System in Japan,' *International Journal of Ethics*, 17, no. 1 (Oct., 1906), 103.

[7] Ben-Ami Shillony, 'Universities and Students in Wartime Japan,' *The Journal of Asian Studies*, 45, no. 4 (Aug., 1986), 769-787. Edgar McVoy, 'Wartime Manpower Controls in Japan,' *American Sociological Review*, 15, no. 4 (Aug., 1950), 534-545

[8] Motoichi Fujita, Tadashi Saito, Hikaru Sato, January 16, 2004.

[9] Frederick S. Hulse, 33.

[10] Motoichi Fujita, Tadashi Saito, Hikaru Sato, January 16, 2004.

[11] 佐藤俊司 (Shunji Sato), '一九四五年七月二十日京ヶ瀬村の一日 (B29 焼山に落つ) July 20, 1945: A Day in Kyōgase Village (The B-29 Downing in Yakeyama),' 村誌 (*Village Historical Record*), 十一月 (November), 平成 14 年 (2002), 150. Valery Burati, 'Fragments of a Mission,' 1972, unpublished manuscript (typewritten), p. 2, George McGraw Private Papers, Gillett, Arkansas.

[12] 'B29 二機撃隊す (Two B-29s Shot Down).' 新潟日報 (*Niigata Nippo*), July 21 1945, sec. Front Page.

[13] Harry George, interview by author, August 24, 2003, notes.

[14] Robert K. Hall, 'Report on Capt. (Now Major) Gordon P. Jordan and Crew, Missing in Action 19/20 July 1945' (San Francisco, California: Sixth Bombardment Group, Office of the Group Intelligence Officer, 15 August, 1945, photocopied), 1-2.

[15] Paul Trump, Lititz, PA, to Hitoshi Fukuda, Questionnaires to B-29 Crewmen Lost over Yokogoshi, Yokogoshi Town Department of History, Yokogoshi, Niigata, Japan.

[16] Lawrence Smith, *9th Bombardment Group (VH) History* (Princeton, NJ: 9th Bomb Group Association, 1995), 338.

[17] However, it also must be pointed out that no corroborating evidence was found to link Gertenbach or any other B-29 from the 9th Bomb Group to this mission. Whether or not he served as a replacement bombardier on this mission, is conjecture, since it is unknown whether 9th Bomb Group airmen were able to serve on 6th Bomb Group missions.

[18] Yoshikazu Nakamura, interview by Toshihide Uemura, July 1, 1998, tape recording, The B-29 Downing Incident (B29 撃墜事件について), Former Yokogōshi City History Department, Yokogōshi, Niigata.

[19] 横越史編さん委員会　(Yokogōshi Town Historical Compilation Committee), comp., *横越町史　(Yokogōshi Town History)* (Niigata: Hokuto, 2003), 745-746.

[20] Robert K. Hall, 'Report on Capt. (Now Major) Gordon P. Jordan and Crew, Missing in Action 19/20 July 1945' (San Francisco, California: Sixth Bombardment Group, Office of the Group Intelligence Officer, 15 August, 1945, photocopied), 1-2. Jay Martin, e-mail to author, September 29, 2006.

[21] Shoichi Kuga, interview by Toshihide Uemura, July 1, 1998, tape recording, The B-29 Downing Incident (B29 撃墜事件について), Former Yokogōshi City History Department, Yokogōshi, Niigata.

[22] Harry E. Steen, interview by Charles Roland, September, 1992, interview HCM 11-92, transcript, Oral History Archives, Hannah Chair for the History of Medicine, McMaster University, Hamilton, Ontario.

[23] Masao Saito, interview by Toshihide Uemura, July 1, 1998, tape recording, The B-29 Downing Incident (B29 撃墜事件について), Former Yokogōshi City History Department, Yokogōshi, Niigata.

[24] Motoichi Fujita, Tadashi Saito, Hikaru Sato, January 16, 2004.

[25] 金塚友之丞 (Tomoyuki Kanazuka), '横越村焼山へ落ちた B29 と京ヶ瀬村へ降りた落下傘 (The B-29 that went down in Yokogōshi and those who parachuted into Kyōgase),' *郷土新潟 (Hometown Niigata)* 6 (February, 1965), 11.

[26] 金塚友之丞 (Tomoyuki Kanazuka), 12.

[27] Yoshikazu Nakamura, July 1, 1998.

[28] Miyo Meguro, interview by Toshihide Uemura, July 1, 1998, tape recording, The B-29 Downing Incident (B29 撃墜事件について), Former Yokogōshi City History Department, Yokogōshi, Niigata. Chuzo Sato, interview by Toshihide Uemura, July 1, 1998, tape recording, The B-29 Downing Incident (B29 撃墜事件について), Former Yokogōshi City History Department, Yokogōshi, Niigata.

[29] Even sixty years later, people of Kyōgase are least likely to talk about what happened next. The subject is taboo to outsiders, foreign or Japanese.

[30] 佐藤俊司 (Shunji Sato), 152.

CHAPTER SEVEN

CAPTURE OF THE JORDAN CREW

Four days before their final mission, the Jordan Crew had sat in on a lecture about escape and evasion.[1] They were told that, as tall Caucasians, there would be little chance of hiding out on Japan's heavily populated islands. Although there was no clear indication about whether the Japanese took prisoners, their safest option would still be to seek out and surrender to the military. Based upon intelligence gathered concerning the fate of flyers downed during the Dresden incendiary attacks, and from what could be extrapolated from the Japanese propaganda broadcasts, they should assume that the civilian population would want to kill them.

The organizers of the lecture either did not know or had never thought about teaching the crews any Japanese phrases to help them to surrender if shot down. The underlying message throughout was that if a crewman went down over Japan, he was on his own. The chances for survival would be slim.

In one of the few formal studies on this topic, E. Paul Torrance interviewed seventy-five crewmen who had bailed out over Japan during the Second World War. He identified two key factors that contributed to their survival. One was if the air commander had maintained communication with the crew so that they could mentally prepare to bail out. The other was if the group had the common goal of helping each other survive once they were on the ground. Crewmen who were separated from their comrades after touching down had the highest probability of panicking. Once a crewman panicked, it was usually only a short time before he would give up the will to survive.[2] In my own research of the accounts of B-29 survivors I found that, if a crewman refrained from using his weapons and maintained a calm demeanor once on the ground, there was a far greater chance of him surviving civilian attacks. Crewmen who cried out in pain or revealed strong emotions such as anger or fear only increased the ferocity of attacks. Those who lost their nerve and resorted to using their firearms to ward off civilians almost always signed their own death warrant.

Jordan had done his best to keep his crew updated about what was happening, though it did seem that Spero had been left out of the loop – a common occurrence for B-29 rear gunners during both the Second World War and the Korean War. However, panic had gripped the crew as soon as the bailout order came. The crew began to fragment and it became every man for himself.

As the crewmen drifted down to the rice paddies below the men became separated. Alone in the night, each would be tested on what he had remembered from his briefings. He would have to face up to what he had said to others during those drinking parties in Jordan's Quonset hut. The manner in which each man responded to what would happen in the next few hours would determine whether he lived or died.

Individual Accounts

Most of the crew landed close to the Agano River along the Uetsu Railway Line.[3] This whole area today is still a wide flood plain filled with lush rice paddies and green garden plots. Most of the trees had long been cut down, although a stretch of pine trees had been left to act as a screen against the harsh winds that lashed the fields during the winter. Except for a few barns and hamlets, there were only a few tiny buildings visible in the distance. Beyond this, the mountains lay over thirty kilometers away. It was near the end of the rainy season, and the rice stalks had grown tall enough for one to squat down in the muck and hide. This would only work until daytime, however, as one would only need to walk along the rows of a rice paddy to find anyone crouching there. For the Jordan Crew, hiding in a rice paddy was like hiding an elephant in a wheat field.

The farmlands surrounding Yakeyama in the autumn of 1944. Nearly a year later the Jordan Crew would land approximately one kilometer from the location of this photo. (Photo courtesy of the Niigata Municipal Department of Cultural History.)

McGraw, Wiernik and Jordan landed within a close vicinity of each other. While McGraw and Wiernik scattered to find cover, Jordan sat quietly on the ground. He pulled his parachute over his head, lit a cigarette, and waited. A group of veterans and firemen approached to see the eerie light of Jordan's cigarette glowing under the parachute. When they got closer, Jordan stood up

84

slowly, stomped out his cigarette, and raised his hands.[4] McGraw and Wiernik both ran when they were spotted and both were captured after a chase. They were all tied up, blindfolded, and escorted back to the Kyōgase Village Hall.[5] On the way, they were ambushed by a crowd of female villagers whose sons had been killed serving in the Army and Navy. They rushed in, stabbing at the crewmen's heads with their spears or trying to hit them in the head with stones.[6] Eventually their captors were able to squeeze them through this gauntlet and into the village hall.

When Trump bailed out, he looked around and saw the three parachutes below him to his left. He tried to move over to their position by dumping air from one side of his parachute. He pulled too hard, and fell several hundred feet like a rock until he could regain control of his descent. He remembered from looking at his navigation map just before jumping that they were over a river. He now looked below and could see fog. After all of this, he wasn't going to drown in the river by getting tangled in his parachute. About ten meters above the fog he hit the emergency release to fall from his harness into what he thought would be water. He miscalculated. As he plummeted, he realized that the fog had concealed the tops of trees, and he landed waist deep in a marshy rice paddy.

He didn't know how fortunate he had been. Sixty years later, when I told Trump's story to villagers in Yakeyama, one of the farmers, Hikaru Sato, became very animated. He was certain that this was his field, and he knew the exact place where Trump must have landed. He stated that if Trump had come down a few meters in any other direction, he would have landed in much harder, shallower paddies that would not have cushioned a fall from such a height.[7]

Trump struggled to free himself from the muck and gathered up his parachute before stuffing it into the rice paddy. At that moment men ran by carrying hand-cranked flashlights. Trump lay low, concealed by the fog and darkness as they passed. They had been so close that he could have reached out and touched them. After some time, Trump ventured out of the paddy to get his bearings. Suddenly he heard a train approach. He realized that he was next to a train track and in the fog he fumbled back to the relative safety of the rice paddy while the freight train rumbled past. It was then that he heard small arms fire – six shots in rapid succession, followed by the most bone-chilling screams that he could have imagined. Mixed with the screams he heard angry voices. They were close. The screams and crying persisted. Now there were more screams off in the distance. Any hope that Trump had of being taken alive had been crushed. The screams were evidence enough that the Japanese weren't taking prisoners. Listening to the cries and then feeble moans of pain wafting through the darkness was so horrifying that Trump pulled out his .45 and put it next to his temple. It seemed far easier to end it now, quickly, rather than to sit and wait passively for the slow, brutal death that was to come.[8]

In the rice paddy that night, Trump faced his own personal Gethsemane. After great personal struggle, he decided that it wouldn't be right to die by his own hand. He pushed the handgun as deep as he could into the paddy mud and promised himself that, when the time came to face his captors, he would neither retaliate nor allow himself to scream out in pain.[9]

Grant was parachuting to the ground when his emergency life raft began to inflate unexpectedly. He couldn't help but feeling that he looked a bit ridiculous coming down over dry ground with a raft bobbing up and down below him. After touching down, he punctured the raft with his survival knife, crammed the parachute and raft into a ditch on the side of a small road, and looked around. He had landed on the edge of what looked like an endless stretch of rice paddies. He ripped off his Mae West lifejacket and paused as he felt the .45 in its holster.

He quickly decided that he wasn't going to wage his own personal war against Japan and threw both the knife and pistol as hard as he could into the rice paddies. Then he scrabbled around and found a culvert under the road. Grant had just crawled in when he heard gunfire and screams. It sounded like Spero, though because of the darkness, he could not be completely certain.[10] Then Grant heard more gunfire, this time much closer, and the sounds of someone being savagely beaten. He hunkered down in the shadows of the culvert, and waited for his turn.[11]

Burkle landed near the railroad and was just gathering up his parachute when a group of civil defense wardens spotted him. They began to chase him down the railroad. He stopped, pulled out his .45, and pointed it in the direction of his pursuers. Everyone froze. Then other villagers began to pour in from other directions. Burkle realized it was over. He threw his .45 into a nearby ditch and raised his hands in surrender. The villagers, infuriated by the standoff, began to beat him and then pulled him along with ropes and *tobikuchi* until they came to a nearby tree used for hanging rice stalks in the harvest season. They fashioned a noose, put it around his neck, and were preparing to lynch him when national guardsmen broke through the crowd. One calmly walked up to Burkle, took the noose off of his neck, and after tying his hands behind his back and affixing a blindfold, escorted Burkle to the Kyōgase Village Hall.[12]

On the way there, a group of women approached Burkle. One elderly lady, known in the area as Grandma Hasegawa, hobbled up and bashed Burkle on the head with a stick. The soldiers stopped and looked at her as if to demand an explanation. She replied, 'I had my child killed in the war. I can't soothe my feelings unless I do something like this.'[13]

Teitaro Sato, an official from another nearby village called Suibara, wrote an account in his later years about the role he played in the capture of another member of the Jordan Crew.

I called out and led *keibo-dan* members and went to hunt for the soldiers who had bailed out. It was pitch black outside because of the air defense alert. The use of flashlights was not allowed either. We came to the marsh, which goes by the name of Maeda, when we heard some angry profane outbursts ahead of us: 'Sit down, you bastard!' 'If you don't do what you're told, we'll beat you hard!' As we got closer, we saw two guys hanging on both of the shoulders of a giant man of about two meters high, and a crowd of people were shouting 'Sit down!' We asked the folks what had happened. They said that the soldier had come down with his parachute on. He was found by villagers drenched to the skin and shivering in the early morning cold. They were having difficulty trying to move this big man. So I decided to talk to this man using my poor English, though it felt very uncomfortable speaking the enemy language that was banned by the authorities. When I said, 'Sit down', in English, the American sat down with no resistance. I asked, 'you name', but he didn't seem to understand my English. So I wrote numbers from 18 to 25 in my notebook, and asked, 'you age', by pointing to each number to him. He lightly nodded at the number 22. I said, 'Stand up', and he stood up straight. Two of my men held his arms tightly, and other *keibo-dan* members surrounded him. He was so tall, none of us were as tall as the height of his shoulders. When I patted his shoulder and said, 'Go', he began to walk quietly. So early in the morning mist, a dark crowd of people somberly made their way toward Kyōgase's Village Hall. It was daybreak when we got to Kyōgashima, passing through Sekiya.[14] It seemed that all the villagers learned about the B29er as they began their morning work. There were a lot of people on the road. Since Kyōgashima was famous for its quality bamboo, old women tried to avenge the deaths of their sons and housewives attempted to avenge the deaths of their husbands, and attacked the B29er over our heads with bamboo poles. Since he was very tall, he got severely injured in the head. He was bleeding from his head. I shouted to stop. I couldn't keep back the people, who were overwrought with rage. We squeezed our way through the throng into the Kyōgase Village Hall with the B29er, our heads covered with his blood.[15]

Just after sunrise crewmen and villagers both reported hearing more incidences of small arms fire. Dickerson had floated further northeast than the rest of his crewmates. When discovered by villagers he drew his .45 and held them at bay by firing over their heads. He was completely surrounded by a throng of people who were now livid with murderous rage.[16] A band of soldiers, led by an officer, entered the crowd and calmly waited until Dickerson had emptied his weapon. One soldier then walked up to Dickerson, holding his hand out for the gun.[17] At this point, Dickerson flashed a glance so full of hatred and menace that it was burned into the memory of those who witnessed it. The soldier didn't budge and continued to hold out his hand in silence. Finally, Dickerson gave up his weapon, being very careful to hand it to the soldier with the barrel pointed away.[18] The soldier took the gun. He turned Dickerson around as if to restrain him, but instead pushed him savagely into the crowd of villagers, and watched in silence while the villagers exacted their punishment.[19] Then the soldiers ordered the villagers to stop as Dickerson was blindfolded, bound, and taken to the Niigata 5B POW Camp.[20]

At Niigata 5B he was interrogated by an officer wearing a light gray uniform with red insignia, who Dickerson described as tall and looking 'very much like an Italian with dark, wavy hair.'[21] This is similar to the description given by Kenneth Cambon, a former POW at Niigata 5B, of the notorious camp commandant Tetsutaro Kato, who only a day earlier had personally executed an American prisoner who had tried to escape the camp.[22] Cambon wrote about sneaking over to Dickerson's holding cell to speak briefly with him before he was taken to Niigata City.

One plane was shot down and a survivor was brought into camp before being sent to Tokyo. He was isolated in a cage near the guardhouse, a small jail within a jail so to speak. I managed to speak to him and get some of the latest news. It appeared that an invasion was imminent. He couldn't believe how strange we all looked and the odd clothes we were wearing, as he could see the work parties going out each day. I only hope he was not later beheaded as some pilots were, even as late as one day before the capitulation.[23]

The sun had risen and it was getting brighter. Trump saw a group of villagers gathering at the corner of the rice paddy where he had been hiding. He had been spotted. Realizing that escape was impossible he raised his hands and sloshed his way towards them. Villagers remember the event too, except they add that he was begging for mercy.[24] This moment of vulnerability nearly cost Trump his life. When he got to the edge of the rice paddy one man approached with a *tobikuchi* and attempted to rip out Trump's throat. Trump held his chin low and fended off further attacks as another man and several women began making thrusts with their spears and *tobikuchi* towards his face and eyes. Then they all rushed in at the same time, knocked him down, and began to stomp on him. They held his legs apart and allowed the women to take turns kicking his groin.

Trump was bleeding and sliding into shock and unconsciousness. He dimly remembered seeing a soldier rushing up to stop the villagers. He pointed to Trump's lieutenant's insignia and held up one finger as he shouted something in explanation to the incensed villagers. Trump thought from the gesture that maybe there was at least one other officer who had survived after all. He recalled vaguely being blindfolded and put into a truck. In spite of what had just happened he carried with him one secret victory. He had endured the beating and had not retaliated or cried out in pain while being kicked.[25]

Several groups had walked over Grant's culvert, unaware that he was hiding below. Eventually someone thought of looking into the culvert. They shone torches inside and saw Grant. The villagers shouted to others, who came with *tobikuchi*. They used these to hook Grant and pull him out. Then they swarmed all over him, beating him mercilessly with their farm implements. Grant was breathing hard and barely conscious when he remembered a soldier driving off the villagers. Grant pulled himself to his feet, dazed, when someone from behind hit him on the back of the head, knocking him out cold.[26]

When he came to, Grant found himself in a makeshift cell at the Kyōgase Village Hall. He was shackled to a concrete pillar as he awaited interrogation.[27] First Lieutenant Koyama, 2nd Lt. Kanki, Warrant Officer Yasuhara, Sgt. Majors Fukutani and Ozaki, and a Corporal Yukio Sugano had arrived from the Niigata Headquarters of the *kempei-tai* to collect the prisoners.[28] Koyama attempted to interrogate several of the prisoners using his broken English, but all were still in a state of shock. Most were unable to speak. However, Koyama wanted answers. Memories about the next several hours are sketchy, except for numb recollections of cursing, shouting, crying, sickening thuds from further beatings, and of sitting in uncomfortable positions while being interrogated with a flashlight shining in their eyes.[29]

The POW Experience

The memoirs of Allied POWs frequently highlight that their treatment in Japan was cruel and sadistic, while the treatment of Japanese POWs sent to the States was humane. They point to statistics showing the high rate of Allied POW deaths in Japan as compared to the extremely low death rate of Allied POWs in German camps, and to the lower rate of death of Japanese POWs held in American detention centers. On the surface, the data is accurate, but a deeper understanding of other factors is necessary to avoid coming to the wrong conclusion.

The Second World War witnessed atrocities against POWs on all sides of the conflict, both during and immediately following the official cessation of hostilities. Britain and Germany became involved in a tit-for-tat exchange of shackling POWs in 1942. The status of Italian POWs was changed to that of Italian Military Internees and they remained prisoners even when Italy began fighting on the side of the Allied powers. German and Russian treatment of each other's prisoners was especially brutal. Most Russians were killed rather than captured, and those who did survive died by the hundreds of thousands from starvation or disease.[30] Hundreds of thousands of Japanese POWs died in Russian gulags after the war. Some survivors were not released until the 1950s. America and Britain changed the status of German POWs to that of Disarmed Enemy Forces immediately after the war, and kept them enclosed in neglected conditions that resulted in the death of several thousand from starvation. Several hundred more died as forced laborers sent to clean up land mines and other dangerous war materials.[31]

It was common knowledge that Japanese military indoctrination stressed that an honorable warrior should never let himself be taken alive. During America's Pacific struggle with Japan, most fought to the bitter end. American troops frequently killed Japanese soldiers outright rather than risk trying to take any as prisoner. The result was that in comparison to the Allied POWs captured by Japanese forces during the early months of the Pacific Theater, the numbers of Japanese troops taken as Prisoners of War were relatively few. MacKenzie found that three dynamics determined the conditions of POWs during the Second World War, regardless of the side on which they fought.[32] These were:

- The availability of resources (food, medicine, etc.) in the captor country.
- The degree to which enemy soldiers felt a measure of affinity towards each other, be it cultural, religious, linguistic, racial or ideological.
- The fear of reciprocity; meaning that apprehension about abuses being meted out on their own POWs kept some captor countries from treating enemy POWs in an inhumane manner.

From an Anglo-American perspective, atrocities committed in German POW camps were fewer because the German High Command feared that similar measures would be taken against their own soldiers. Abuses on both sides were also somewhat mitigated by the cultural, religious and racial similarities between combatants. In the Pacific, however, both sides had taken great pains to demonize the other and to highlight how alien they were, both culturally and racially.

Japanese Treatment of POWs

Japan's history of dealing with POWs has been decidedly mixed. For much of its past, the treatment of captives could be summarized as 'crush the enemy'. During its civil war for example, POWs were executed as soon as possible.[33] Gordon Daniels records that the British doctor, William Willis, who in 1868 had been sent as an observer with the Imperial Army during their campaign in Niigata, repeatedly chided military leaders in a manner that was to be echoed by Western diplomats throughout the remainder of the 19th century:

> If Britain wanted a Japanese government to amend its policies or institutions there was one simple technique – to appeal to its pride. The Japanese were told that 'all the great countries of the world would hear with horror' of their present ways; while the steps Britain proposed would be described as noble, modern, enlightened, and likely to raise the reputation of Japan in the councils of the world.[34]

In large part the Japanese government took these criticisms to heart and, drawing from the teachings of Bushido, the policy towards POWs became, as most famously expressed by Emperor Meiji, 'crush the enemy for the sake of the nation, but never forget to have mercy.'[35] As a result, Japan's treatment of Russian POWs during the Russo-Japanese War and German POWs during the First World War was so humane that it won international praise in the councils of the world. This was during a time when the 'civilized' nations of Europe were committing atrocities against captured soldiers from both sides of the trenches.[36]

In the period leading up to the Second World War, however, the sweeping changes instituted in Japanese society by racist ultra-nationalists resulted in 'a military system that placed little value on the lives of foreign natives or prisoners and, in the final stages of the war, even on those of the Japanese themselves.'[37] The policy for POWs under this regime could be best phrased as 'a crushed enemy will be shown no mercy.'

This was the situation in which the Jordan Crew had landed. They had parachuted into an enemy nation where, because of Operation Starvation, there was little food or medicine. The crew and their captors had virtually no known cultural, racial, linguistic or religious bridges of commonality. There was little fear of reciprocity, since Japanese POWs were considered by their military leaders as cowards worthy of death, and the populace had been encouraged to direct their hatred and frustrations towards these demons who had had the audacity to try and escape their burning B-29. Villagers knew that the Americans would soon be coming in force, and for a few moments they would have to confront the invaders with bamboo spears before embracing death. Now was the last chance to exact some revenge.

The Transfer to Niigata City

Sometime in the mid-morning the prisoners were transferred to Niigata City. Yukio Sugano had scrounged around earlier to find a truck large enough to transport all of the crewmen.[38] The truck pulled up with Sugano and four other soldiers in the back. Residents of Kyōgase milled around outside the town hall waiting to catch a sight of the crewmen. Local firefighters were still boasting about their bravery in capturing some of the crewmen.[39] Everyone's attention turned as the doors of the village hall opened and Warrant Officer Yasunara escorted each of the seven members of the Jordan Crew out to the truck.

George McGraw as he left the Kyōgase Village Hall for Transport to Niigata.
(Photo courtesy of George McGraw/Val Burati.)

Many of the crewmen seemed tired and frightened. Some of the villagers giggled with amusement since it appeared that a number of crewmen had lost control of their bodily functions during the night.[40] The soldiers roughly lugged each crewman onto the flatbed. Jordan, who had maintained his taciturn and stoic attitude, was the last to walk out of the building. Walking as tall as he could, Jordan exuded an air of dignity, and won some admiration from eyewitnesses.[41]

Jordan Crew in Kyōgase being loaded in a truck for transfer to Niigata City.
(Photo courtesy of George McGraw/Val Burati.)

After this some eyewitnesses remember one crewman being either dragged or carried out of the hall. He had deep cuts on the right back side of his neck, was covered with blood, and seemed to be unconscious.[42] One observer, Shunji Sato, remarked that this crewman was thrown in the back of the truck, 'like cords of wood', and then was covered with a rough canvas sheet, though some thought that something like a sack had been put over his head. Sato learned later that this crewman had died.[43]

Shunkichi Shimizu, the photographer from the local Niigata newspaper, had just arrived on the scene with another *kempei-tai* officer by the name of Kawashima.[44] He snapped a few photos of the Jordan Crew as they were being loaded into the truck, and then left to view the crash site.

Jordan and his crew were scheduled to be transported to the Niigata Headquarters. Between Kyōgase and Niigata, however, the truck stopped first in Yakeyama, where Sugano and other soldiers carried the body of the dead crewman back to the crash site.[45] Keiichi Meguro, the Village Ward for Yakeyama, had accompanied the truck from Kyōgase back to Yakeyama. Villagers in Yakeyama were kept away from the prisoners as the truck made its way to Kameda. The truck stopped again, this time in front of the City Hall so that one of the soldiers could go inside and call ahead to headquarters. It should be noted that observers in Yakeyama and Kameda both mention there being six crewmen in the truck.[46] The significance of this point will become apparent later.

Jordan Crew as they leave for Niigata City. A careful study of the picture shows six crewmen in the truck. A seventh crewman is believed to be under the white sheet in the back.
(Photo courtesy of George McGraw/Val Burati.)

While the truck was parked in Kameda, a crowd of curious onlookers gathered. Two elderly ladies by the names of Suzuki and Kitagami, who lived above a tofu shop from across the street, approached the blindfolded crewmen. Kitagami's daughter and grandchildren had been boiled to death in the Sumida River during the Tokyo fire-bombings. Suzuki and Kitagami came up to the truck. One of them wielded a saw and attempted to attack the crewmen. The soldiers in the truck prevented the ladies from hurting the crewmen, but not without some difficulty. As the women were carried away kicking and screaming, variations of what they said entered into local folklore.

> Let me cut off their heads as they are detestable fellows. Four of my sons are already dead at the front![47]

And as Kitagami was dragged away, she was heard to say:

> 'They killed my grandchildren! I will never have peace until I have avenged their deaths!'[48]

Village storytellers often recall feelings of bitter tragedy when they recount the tale of these angry ladies. Their words are remembered because they represented the feelings of many women, young and old, and it was their justification for why they had attacked the crewmen during their capture. While understanding how they felt, there was also an underlying message about how war changes the best of us for the worst. No one wanted or expected to hear such violent words coming from the lips of a kindly grandmother. In Japan, as elsewhere, grandmothers are a bastion of gentleness and love. Seeing these old ladies lashing out with murderous intent cooled the passions of the younger hotheads and filled many with pity. These grandmothers had seen the end of their families. There would be no days of indulging their grandchildren, or of giving wise advice to the young. No one would pray for them at the altar of the ancestors when they died. The truck pulled off for Niigata and many returned home with complex feelings that, even today, they find difficult to express.

Niigata Interrogations

Owing to a lack of space, Jordan and Trump were taken to the headquarters of the *kempei-tai* near Niigata's West Port while the rest were kept at the Niigata City Central Police Station on the other side of the Shinano River. Dickerson was brought to the police station later, returning the group's number back to seven.

They were again interrogated by officers of the *kempei-tai*. This time, there were also officers from the Navy and the local Anti-aircraft Corps present. Some could speak English quite well. But they directed their questions through an interpreter by the surname of Hiromasa, who had been an English teacher at Niigata High School before the war.[49] When the blindfolds were removed, several members of the Jordan Crew remembered being surprised at the appearance of the officers who were calmly sitting behind desks and preparing to interrogate them. These men were tall, muscular, well-fed, and in much better physical shape than the diminutive villagers who had captured them earlier.[50]

Japanese military traditions during this era were highly ritualized, reflecting the idealized forms of conduct that had stretched back for centuries. The interrogation was one such ritual. While many *kempei-tai* interrogations amounted to little more than intimidation and beatings from uniformed thugs, the ideal ritual nevertheless remained strong in the minds of those who were in Japanese law enforcement.

Each crewman was required to sit with his legs folded under him in the Japanese *seiza* style. He was to look downward in an effort to demonstrate a spirit of *hansei*, an attitude of regretful self-reflection upon one's past crimes and of a desire to come clean. The interrogators would ask questions to which they already knew the answers, and use these to test the sincerity of the prisoner. All answers were to be given in humility and complete honesty as part of the process of the prisoner's purification. At the end, prisoners should admit their guilt and bravely accept the administration of punishment. If the prisoner had shown a deep level of sincerity then the captors might show some small measure of mercy, though none should be expected for confessing to one's crimes.

The experience of the Jordan Crew during these interrogations depended upon how they unknowingly conformed to the expected norms of this ritual. The attitudes of most were misinterpreted as openly defiant and they were beaten until they provided answers to, what seemed at the time, mundane questions about their outfit, current events in America, the types of mines they had dropped, their plane's capabilities, and so on. However, Trump's quiet, respectful attitude impressed his interrogators. He endured the pain of sitting *seiza*-style well and received an expression of mercy – after the formal interrogation had finished. He was offered a chair and allowed to sit for awhile until he could recover the feeling in his legs.[51]

The wreck of the Daikoku-Maru in Niigata's West Port on July 21, 1945.
(Photo courtesy of the Niigata Municipal Department of Cultural History.)

Results of the Mining Mission and Reports from the Crashsite

During these interrogations, everyone was startled by an explosion from only about 500 meters away in the nearby harbor. The Daikoku-maru, a dredger named after the Japanese god of industry, was working in Niigata's delta when it had been hit by one of the mines dropped earlier in the night. McGraw recalls the thrill of retribution that he felt upon hearing this explosion. While the seven men sat in their cells awaiting interrogation, another seven men, including the captain, were dying in the harbor as their boat went down.[52] Another explosion was heard soon afterwards. The Daiji-maru, a cargo ship carrying a load of iron ore, was severely damaged.[53] On the docks of the Marutsu Company, Allied POWs watched the scene with glee. They would have less work today.[54]

All of the crewmen in the Niigata offices had been separated and blindfolded when transported. While they knew that others in their group had survived, nobody knew who or how many. In the afternoon, some *kempei-tai* officers returned from the crash site, and through the interpreter, provided bits of information to the crew about their comrades who had died that night.

Jordan was told that the pilot had died an honorable death by going down with the plane. From their description he assumed this must have been Hawkins. Officers also told Jordan that two in his crew had fought back with their weapons and couldn't be taken alive. Another was reported to have died when his parachute didn't open up in time. Jordan had doubts about this last story because the interrogating officer added that Jordan would be reported as suffering the same fate if he did not fully cooperate with the interrogation.[55]

The other crewmen were told variations of the same theme. Some had died in the plane and some were killed. Similar stories were told to the POWs in Niigata 5B by guards who had been out looking for the Jordan Crew. As will be seen later, these stories were in stark contrast to what was reported after the war to investigators assigned to the American Occupation Forces in Niigata.

The Train to Tokyo

Late in the afternoon the Jordan Crew was again blindfolded and driven to Niigata's train station. Police and soldiers worked hard to keep the crush of the crowd from further injuring the crew. In addition to the loss of the Daikoku-maru earlier that afternoon, they had not forgotten about the mine that had killed several local schoolchildren only a couple of weeks earlier.

The crew was put on a passenger train to Tokyo with a detachment of sixteen guards. Depending on where the crewman sat on the train, the twelve hour trip to Tokyo was either a brief respite from the terror of the past day, or a continuation of the pain.

Japanese often take the words that describe objects of fear and loathing and turn these into curses, such as in the case of the 1995 Tokyo gas attacks, when high school students would call another person *sarin* (the name of the poisonous gas using in the attacks) as the ultimate insult. Trump remembers that at each station the train stopped, several passengers would bash him on the head, growling '*bee ni-ju ku*' (B-29) as they passed. He had quite a headache by the time they reached Tokyo.[56]

They arrived at Tokyo Station early in the morning of July 21 and were led blindfolded as they walked for thirty minutes to the Tokyo Main Headquarters of the *kempei-tai*, located just across the moat from the Imperial Palace grounds. After they were processed, they were thrown into dark, stinking, overcrowded cells.

---

[1] Florio Spero, July 15, 1945, war diary, Spero Family Collection, Homer Glen, Illinois.

[2] E. Paul Torrance, 'The Behavior of Small Groups Under the Stress Condition of "Survival",' *American Sociological Review* 19, no. 6 (December, 1954), 752, 754-55.

[3] 横越史編さん委員会 (Yokogōshi Town Historical Compilation Committee), comp. 横越町史 (Yokogōshi Town History). Niigata: Hokuto, (2003), 745-746. 佐藤俊司 (Shunji Sato), '一九四五年七月二十日京ヶ瀬村の一日 (B29 焼山に 落つ) July 20, 1945: A Day in

Kyōgase Village (The B-29 Downing in Yakeyama),' 村誌 *(Village Historical Record)*, 十
一月 (November), 平成 14 年 (2002), 152.

[4] Paul Trump, interview by author, September 13, 2004, MD Recording. Robert Grant, interview by author, October 29, 2003, CD Recording.

[5] Benny Doyle Conine Sr. and William Doswell Conine, III, 'Conine Brothers' Early Years,' 2005, unpublished manuscript (photocopy), 269, Family Memoirs, The Woodlands, Texas.

[6] 金塚友之丞 (Tomoyuki Kanazuka), '横越村焼山へ落ちた B29 と京ヶ瀬村へ降りた落下
傘 (The B-29 that went down in Yokogōshi and those who parachuted into Kyōgase),' 郷土新
潟 *(Hometown Niigata)* 6 (February 1965), 14.

[7] Motoichi Fujita, Tadashi Saito, Hikaru Sato, interview by author, January 16, 2004, MD Recording.

[8] Paul Trump, September 13, 2004.

[9] Paul Trump, 'War Memories,' 2003, unpublished manuscript (photocopy), 2, Trump Family Papers, Lititz, PA. Paul Trump, September 13, 2004.

[10] Edmund Steffler (Capt.), 'Missing Air Crew Report #14786' (College Park, Maryland: NARA, 1945, July 23, photocopied).

[11] Robert Grant, interview by author, April 23, 2004, MD Recording.

[12] Paul Trump, interview by author, March 23, 2004, MD Recording. 金塚友之丞 (Tomoyuki Kanazuka), 13-14.

[13] 金塚友之丞 (Tomoyuki Kanazuka), 14.

[14] Because of the meander that nearly separated Yakeyama from Kyōgase into an island, the old name of an area between Yakeyama and Kyōgase was known as Kyōgashima, literally, 'Kyōga Island'. The meander today has been filled in to make farmland and the river has since changed its course.

[15] 佐藤貞太郎 (Teitaro Sato), 'B-29 撃墜余談 (Digressions about the B-29 Downing),' 五頭
郷土文化 *(Gozu Hometown Culture)* 7 (December, 1984), 60-61. Translated by Hiromi Hadley.

[16] 'American soldiers surrounded by spear-wielding villagers (竹やりの村民米兵囲む),' *Niigata Nippo*, August 12, 2000.

[17] Masao Saito, interview by Toshihide Uemura, July 1, 1998, tape recording, The B-29 Downing Incident (B29 撃墜事件について), Former Yokogōshi City History Department, Yokogōshi, Niigata-shi.

[18] 金塚友之丞 (Tomoyuki Kanazuka), 13.

[19] Walter Dickerson, Champaign County, Illinois, Affidavit to War Crimes Office, Civil Affairs Division, October 16, 1947, Private Papers of Robert Neptune, Fiske Hanley Collection, Ft. Worth, Texas.

[20] Toshio Watanabe was a guard at Niigata Camp 5B, and remembers when the B-29 crewman was brought to the camp. As cited in Toshio Watanabe, interview by author, November 8, 2003, Sanjo City, Niigata.

[21] Walter Dickerson, Affidavit to War Crimes Office, Civil Affairs Division, October 16, 1947.

[22] 'Investigation Division Reports #41.' (GHQ/SCAP Records. Record Group 331: National Archives and Records Service, March 1946 - April 1949. NARA, Washington DC, Photocopied). Kenneth Cambon, *Guest of Hirohito* (Vancouver: PW Press, 1990), 85.

[23] Kenneth Cambon, 83-84.

[24] 金塚友之丞 (Tomoyuki Kanazuka), 13-14.

[25] Paul Trump, 'War Memories,' 3.

[26] Robert Grant, April 23, 2004.

[27] 佐藤俊司 (Shunji Sato), 153.

[28] 'Investigation Division Reports #226' (GHQ/SCAP Records. Record Group 331: National Archives and Records Service, March 1946 - April 1948. NARA, Washington DC, photocopied).

[29] Robert Grant, April 23, 2004. Paul Trump, September 13, 2004.

[30] S.P. MacKenzie, 'The Treatment of Prisoners of War in World War II,' *The Journal of Modern History* 66, no. 3 (September 1994), 501-503.

[31] Ambrose Gunter and Stephen Bischof, *Eisenhower and the German POWs: Facts Against Falsehood* (Baton Rouge, LA: Louisiana State University Press, 1992).

[32] S.P. MacKenzie, 508-511.

[33] Gordon Daniels, 'The Japanese Civil War (1868) -- A British View,' *Modern Asian Studies* 1, no 3 (1967), 249.

[34] Gordon Daniels, 252-53.

[35] Carol Gluck, *Japan's Modern Myths* (Princeton, New Jersey: Princeton University Press, 1985), 89.

[36] Charles Burdick and Ursula Moessner, *The German Prisoners-of- War in Japan, 1914-1920* (Lanham, MD: University Press of America, 1984). Phillip A. Towle, 'Japanese Treatment of Prisoners in 1904-1905.' *Military Affairs* 19 (1975), 115-117.

[37] Masao Maruyama, 'Theory and Psychology of Ultranationalism,' in *Thought and Behavior in Modern Japanese Politics*, (Oxford: Oxford University Press, 1963). Haruko Taya Cook and Theodore F. Cook, *Japan at War: An Oral History* (New York: The New Press, 2000), 26.

[38] Yukio Sugano, interview by Toshihide Uemura, July 3, 1998, tape recording, The B-29 Downing Incident (B29 撃墜事件について), Former Yokogōshi City History Department, Yokogōshi, Niigata.

[39] 佐藤俊司 (Shunji Sato), 152

[40] Chuzo Sato, interview by Toshihide Uemura, July 1, 1998, tape recording, The B-29 Downing Incident (B29 撃墜事件について), Former Yokogōshi City History Department, Yokogōshi, Niigata.

[41] Anonymous C, interview by author, December 29, 2003, notes.

[42] 網干嘉一郎 (Kiichiro Amihoshi)'戦時中の記録 (War Memories),' *郷土新潟 (Hometown Niigata)* 6 (February, 1965), 16.

[43] 佐藤俊司 (Shunji Sato), 153.

[44] Valery Burati, 'Fragments of a Mission,' 1972, unpublished manuscript (typewritten), 3, George McGraw Private Papers, Gillett, Arkansas.

[45] Masao Saito, July 1, 1998. Yoshikazu Nakamura, interview by Toshihide Uemura, July 1, 1998, tape recording, The B-29 Downing Incident (B29 撃墜事件について), Former Yokogōshi City History Department, Yokogōshi, Niigata.

[46] Yoshikazu Nakamura, July 1, 1998. 'Investigative Division Reports #472' (GHQ/SCAP Records. Record Group 331, National Archives and Records Service, May 1946 - March 1947. NARA, Washington DC, photocopied).

[47] 'Investigative Division Reports #472.'

[48] 金塚友之亟 (Tomoyuki Kanazuka), 10.

[49] 'Investigation Division Reports #226.'

[50] Robert Grant, April 23, 2004.

[51] Paul Trump, September 13, 2004.

[52] Niigata City Historical Board, comp., *戦場としての新潟 (Battleground Niigata)* (Niigata City: City of Niigata, 1998), 94.

[53] Niigata City Historical Board, 83.

[54] William Howard Chittenden, *From China Marine to Jap POW* (Paducah, Kentucky: Turner Publishing Company, 1995), 168.

[55] Edmund Steffler (Capt.), 'Missing Air Crew Report #14786.'

[56] Paul Trump, September 13, 2004.

CHAPTER EIGHT

CHAOS AT THE CRASH SITE

Oral and written accounts of what happened at the crash site contain many points of similarity and divergence. When I interviewed villagers from the area, most of the time they preferred to speak with me in groups, as they did when talking to Japanese researchers who had studied this incident a few years earlier. The version of events given to me during group meetings was similar to what had been reported earlier to the first American war crimes investigators. However, when the opportunity arose for me to speak with people on an individual basis, away from the eyes of the group, very different tales emerged. Like an archaeologist trying to reconstruct and interpret some ancient artifact, what follows is my attempt to piece together the fragments of the numerous stories about what happened on that day.

Fear, Fire and Rage

The B-29 burned most of the night, while various bands of villagers and local air raid wardens went back and forth from the crash site before daybreak.[1] As the morning light illuminated the smoking wreckage, more and more villagers from Yakeyama and the surrounding area cautiously ventured to the site. They were shocked by the size of the plane's twisted carcass, and retched from the reek of burning rubber that was mingled with charred flesh.[2]

The front of the plane was a burned out shell. They peered inside the cockpit to see a body, mostly cremated, seated and still desperately clutching the elevator controls.[3] Dried blood could still be seen on one of the hands. Depending on the story, either somewhere inside the front of the plane near to the seated corpse or leaning on the wreckage just outside the plane, there was another body that was partially burned. Curiously, some recall that navigation maps had been scattered around.[4] Others remember the body was still wearing a cap and had a .45 either in his hand or near his body. They looked in wonder at his lifeless blue eyes that stared upwards towards the sky.[5]

The *keibō-dan* was only nominally guarding the crash site, so some villagers explored the rear cabin of the plane and ransacked it for anything of value. They found the emergency food stores. Although at first they were afraid to touch it, some took what they could and ran off. It was the first time for many of them to try turkey, butter or cheese, and the memory stayed with them all their lives.[6] Others found fishing tackle and useful items that might be fashioned into tools for work on the farm.

Soldiers and *kempei-tai* officers inspecting the wreckage
of Jordan's B-29 on the morning of July 20, 1945.
(Niigata Nippo, July 21, 1945.)

Sometime later, a group of men came dragging the body of one crewman on a small sled. His hands were tied behind him as if he had been captured, but his legs were burned up to the shins.[7] It was the body of Florio Spero. Not long after this, Sugano and a few soldiers brought the body of the crewman who had been covered by a canvas sheet in the back of the truck with the captured survivors of the Jordan Crew.[8] This body was carried in the sheet and placed on the ground with his equipment and parachute not far from Spero. The body had a broken leg that was twisted around and had horrible wounds on his head and face. This was Adams.

100

The bodies of Adams (foreground) and Spero (background).
(Photo courtesy of George McGraw/Val Burati.)

Pandemonium broke out with the arrival of these two bodies. The *keibō-dan* tried to keep the villagers back, but such was their frenzied rage that they began to beat and abuse the bodies in various ways, such as those who pulled down the pants of Adams and put a sweet potato in his crotch.[9] Others searched the bodies for jewelry or anything else of value.

This was the primal scene that was being acted out when the ranking *kempei-tai* officers arrived. Lt. Colonel Toma ordered the guards to beat back the crowd so that the crash site could be properly investigated. All of the papers, maps and anything else of interest which remained in the plane or that was on the bodies were collected.[10] Then Shunkichi Shimizu took pictures of the debris and of the two bodies that had been brought back to the plane.

Turning on Each Other

The *kempei-tai* officers noticed one woman standing in the crowd who was dressed strangely. She was wearing coveralls and had a wavy hairdo uncommon for Japanese women at the time. She seemed to have a decidedly Western look about her. She wasn't from Yakeyama and, to the eyes of the emotionally-charged villagers, the shabby coveralls that she was wearing looked suspiciously similar to the clothing of the dead B-29 crewmen lying on the ground in front of them. Even more alarming, she was jotting down notes about what was taking place. Some of the people began to jostle her about, shouting that she must be a spy. The officers promptly arrested her and brought her back to Niigata for questioning. As she was carted off, she glared at others with an unabashed look of defiance. She was released soon afterward, but the incident led to the short-lived rumor that one member of the crew had been a woman.[11]

The villagers were told that that their cooperation would soon be required to help remove the wreckage. Guards were posted around the site until the grisly task of removing the bodies could be finished. They pulled the cremated remains out of the cockpit with ropes. They put it and the other body that had been burned into burlap bags.[12] The villagers took sliding doors out of a nearby hut and carried the other two to the village ward offices. There they were bagged and hoisted up in a storage area until later, when the manner in which the corpses should be disposed would be decided.

A Dreary Playground

A couple of days after the crash the guards still milled around Yakeyama but they were not particularly watchful over the plane.[13] What had once been a weapon of war now became a jungle gym for the village children.[14] After the intensity of violence, fear and death that still hung over the field, it seemed somehow necessary to allow the children to purify the place with their laughter and games. Their parents, however, looked worriedly at the fields. Their sweet potato field had been ruined by the B-29, a nearby mulberry grove had been burned by the fire, and the crops in the surrounding fields had been trampled by the feet of crowds who had come to see the crash site. Now they were being required to feed the soldiers who were watching the plane and would soon have to deal with the wreckage of the B-29 instead of gathering the remnants of a harvest that might be scavenged from their troubled fields.

Cleaning up the Mess

Rumors spread that free food would be provided to those who would help in the disposal of the B-29. People from all over the area rushed in to help remove the wreckage.[15] The soldiers and *kempei-tai* officers overseeing the task forced the villagers in Yakeyama and the local branch of the Patriotic Women's Society (*aikoku fujin-kai*) to provide the food they had been hoarding to feed those working in the fields. Later on the villagers sought to recoup some of their losses by putting the remaining wreckage laying in their fields to good use. Plastics from the plane's windshield were burned in lamps to further illuminate their evenings.[16] Pieces of metal were fashioned into paperweights, rulers, and used to patch holes in roofs.[17] Someone found a reservoir of hydraulic fluid in the landing gear and used it as a lubricant. Propellers were kept as souvenirs by Keiichi Meguro, and two machine guns were sent to the elementary school in Yokogōshi as a wall display.[18]

The main fuselage was split into two pieces and loaded onto a truck. Later it was taken to the park in front of Hakusan Shrine, the main Shinto Shrine in the center of Niigata City, and displayed for ten days in an effort to remind people that America was not an invincible enemy. Shunkichi Shimizu expressed the sentiment of many at the time.

We have heard the enemy has thousands of the same planes in the Marianas, but we are ready to crush them. We never worry about them. Whenever they come they will be shot down like this one here.[19]

The wreckage of the B-29 then passed into history. No one remembers what happened to it, though part of it seems to have been sold to a local junk dealer, who scrapped the aluminum and fashioned it into pots and pans.[20] It is likely that most of the wreckage, which contained large amounts of the war material duralumin, made its way to Niigata Iron Works, where it was melted down for the faltering war effort.

As the B-29 went to the furnace, so the hopes of Niigata citizens also melted in the ensuing weeks. Nagaoka to the south was decimated in an incendiary attack on August 1, in which over two-thirds of the city was destroyed and approximately 1400 people were killed. Ironically, Niigata was taken off the secret list of potential atomic bomb targets on August 1, which had previously shielded it from conventional air attacks. The decision to take Niigata off the list of atomic bomb sites was based upon concerns about losing the bomb on the long trip to Niigata, and because the layout of factories and homes in Niigata was unsuitable for such an attack.[21] Dropping the Bomb on Niigata might not have resulted in the psychological effect that the United States government intended to recoup from its investment. Botching the mission could have encouraged the Japanese military to fight on.[22] From the Japanese military's side, Niigata's loss would have been of little consequence since the port was no longer of any practical value to the Empire. Niigata was on its own, and fair game for direct aerial attacks. By the beginning of August, Niigata's harbor came under rocket attack from P-51 fighters, which damaged the petrochemical facilities and crippled a naval frigate that had been docked for repairs. The ship burned for days and could not be approached because of the exploding munitions on board.[23] One way or another, it wouldn't be long now.

---

[1] 佐藤俊司 (Shunji Sato), '一九四五年　七月二十日　京ヶ瀬村の一日（B29 焼山に 落つ）July 20, 1945: A Day in Kyōgase Village (The B-29 Downing in Yakeyama),' 村誌 *(Village Historical Record)*, 十一月 (November), 平成 14 年 (2002), 151.

[2] Yoshikazu Nakamura, interview by Toshihide Uemura, July 1, 1998, tape recording, The B-29 Downing Incident (B29 撃墜事件について), Former Yokogōshi City History Department, Yokogōshi, Niigata.

[3] Masao Saito, interview by Toshihide Uemura, July 1, 1998, tape recording, The B-29 Downing Incident (B29 撃墜事件について), Former Yokogōshi City History Department, Yokogōshi, Niigata.

[4] Valery Burati, 'Fragments of a Mission,' 1972, unpublished manuscript (typewritten), 2-3, George McGraw Private Papers, Gillett, Arkansas.

[5] Miyo Meguro, interview by Toshihide Uemura, July 1, 1998, tape recording, The B-29 Downing Incident (B29 撃墜事件について), Former Yokogōshi City History Department, Yokogōshi, Niigata.

[6] Masao Saito, July 1, 1998.

[7] Anonymous B, interview by author, June 20, 2003, notes. Masao Saito, July 1, 1998.

[8] When interviewed over the phone by historian Toshihide Uemura, Sugano stated unconvincingly that he could not remember the truck stopping in Yakeyama on its way to Niigata, 'But if it did,' he said, 'maybe it was to show that the American soldiers had been captured.' As cited in Yukio Sugano, interview by Toshihide Uemura, July 3, 1998, tape recording, The B-29 Downing Incident (B29 撃墜事件について), Former Yokogōshi City History Department, Yokogōshi, Niigata.

[9] 金塚友之亟 (Tomoyuki Kanazuka), '横越村焼山へ落ちた B29 と京ヶ瀬村へ降りた落下傘 (The B-29 that went down in Yokogōshi and those who parachuted into Kyōgase),' 郷土新潟 (Hometown Niigata) 6 (February, 1965), 11.

[10] John Reitze (2nd Lt.), 'Report of Recovery Team 1 (T1J27-141)' (HQ Eighth Army APO 343, Memorial Branch, Quartermaster General, 1946, photocopied).

[11] Yoshikazu Nakamura, July 1, 1998.

[12] Masao Saito, July 1, 1998.

[13] Masao Saito, July 1, 1998.

[14] Motoichi Fujita,, Tadashi Saito, Hikaru Sato, interview by author, January 16, 2004, MD Recording.

[15] Masao Saito, July 1, 1998. Shoichi Kuga, interview by Toshihide Uemura, July 1, 1998, tape recording, The B-29 Downing Incident (B29 撃墜事件について), Former Yokogōshi City History Department, Yokogōshi, Niigata. 佐藤貞太郎 (Teitaro Sato), 'B-29 撃墜余談 (Digressions about the B-29 Downing),' 五頭郷土文化 (Gozu Hometown Culture) 7 (December, 1984), 63-65.

[16] Yoshikazu Nakamura, July 1, 1998.

[17] Masao Saito, July 1, 1998.

[18] Chuzo Sato, interview by Toshihide Uemura, July 1, 1998, tape recording, The B-29 Downing Incident (B29 撃墜事件について), Former Yokogōshi City History Department, Yokogōshi, Niigata. Shoichi Kuga, July 1, 1998.

[19] Valery Burati, 3.

[20] Masao Saito, July 1, 1998. Kyomi Shimizu, interview by Toshihide Uemura, July 1, 1998, tape recording, The B-29 Downing Incident (B29 撃墜事件について), Former Yokogōshi City History Department, Yokogōshi, Niigata.

[21] 509th Composite Group, 'Atomic Bomb Missions' (San Francisco: Commanding General, USASTAF, APO 234, 1945. Archived at Osaka: Osaka International Peace Center, photocopied), 40-42.

[22] Jim B. Smith and Malcolm McConnell, The Last Mission: The Secret Story of World War II's Final Battle (New York: Broadway Books, 2003), 100.

[23] Niigata City Historical Board, comp., 戦場としての新潟 (Battleground Niigata) (Niigata City: City of Niigata, 1998), 83. William Howard Chittenden, From China Marine to Jap POW (Paducah, Kentucky: Turner Publishing Company, 1995), 169-170.

CHAPTER NINE

IN THE PRISON OF THE *KEMPEI-TAI*

The main headquarters of the *kempei-tai* was one of the few buildings left standing in central Tokyo. Downed airmen were actually prisoners of the Japanese Eastern Army. But, because of a shortage of staff who could speak English, the airmen were transferred into the custody of the military police. The *kempei-tai* had English-speaking personnel and were skilled at breaking prisoners both physically and mentally during the process of extracting information.[1] Jordan and his crew stayed for only three weeks in this prison, but the experience left a lifetime of psychological scars on each of them.

In retaliation for the fire-bombing campaign earlier that year, the status of captured B-29 crewmen had been changed to that of a *hokaku beihei*, sometimes translated into English as a 'Special Prisoner'. The Japanese word carries the meaning of an American soldier who has violated the expected rules of engagement, and therefore has forfeited any rights or privileges that might have been afforded to him as a regular POW.[2] Each member of the Jordan Crew was forced to sign documents stating that they had willingly confessed to crimes against humanity for the bombing of innocent civilians. Once all of the crew had signed these papers they were no longer considered POWs. They were now unlawful combatants sitting on death row.

The Imperial Japanese Military Police

The *kempei-tai* were an elite military police unit that had been formed in the 1880s. Originally they were responsible for military law enforcement. But later their powers were extended so that they could ferret out soldiers who harbored pacifist thoughts or other non-conformist attitudes. During the 1930s, with the rise of fascism and virtual military rule that had ended Japan's fledgling Taishō Democracy, Hideki Tōjō and other rising stars within the military aristocracy secured broad discretionary powers for the organization. As a natural consequence of the slogan, 'every citizen a soldier', the reach of the *kempei-tai* began to stretch to every area of citizens' lives. Travel, labor, rationing, propaganda, and broadcasting were just part of their domain. The *kempei-tai* were also in charge of several black projects, such as Unit 731 in Manchuria, which developed biological weapons and tested their effectiveness on prisoners taken from the local populace; the secret island facility of Okunoshima, which produced chemical weapons for the war effort in China and Southeast Asia; and a uranium enrichment program which sought to create a Japanese atomic bomb.[3]

In order both to maintain homeland security and protect Japan from foreign insurgents, the *kempei-tai* regularly spied on citizens through wiretaps, bugs, and a far-reaching network of informants. Anyone who might have been influenced by non-Japanese ideas was kept under constant surveillance: Communists, Christians who had not bowed to the Emperor, pacifists, Korean agitators, and even former English teachers. A military police officer was empowered to arrest any soldier of lower rank. As the lowest-ranking soldiers of Japan's army, ordinary citizens were at the mercy of even the most junior officer in the *kempei-tai*. Stories of abuse and torture became so commonplace that the practices were begrudgingly accepted as customary.

With the war effort going from bad to worse, the subsequent cost of keeping discontent under control proved to be a staggering burden for the military government. In 1942, the number of *kempei-tai* personnel was around 3,600. By 1945, the number had swelled to over 70,000.[4] The increase created considerable friction with the local police departments. The police saw the *kempei-tai* as heavy-handed and cruel. The *kempei-tai* viewed the local police as corrupt and incompetent bumpkins. Civilians feared them both. During the capture of the Jordan Crew police from the local Kyōgase and Niigata departments were always on hand, but they were there mainly as a formality. The *kempei-tai* were in charge, and everyone knew it.

Prison Staff

Other *kempei-tai* offices in Tokyo had long been destroyed by the time of the Jordan Crew's arrival. Most of these soldiers and staff had been sent to the outlying areas to keep an eye on the fleeing populace. At least thirty members of Tokyo's offices were sent to Niigata after the March 1945 Tokyo fire-bombings and were rotated back and forth between Tokyo and Niigata in small squads.[5] The Jordan Crew recognized several of the men who captured them doing guard duty in Tokyo during their incarceration.[6]

Those who were recruited for the military police typically came from conservative backgrounds. Being free from dangerous, un-Japanese thoughts, they knew very little about the outside world, let alone a foreign language. Japanese students who had studied abroad or Japanese who had lived for some time in the United States or the British Empire were recruited as interpreters and handlers. These were the people who had the most contact with B-29 crewmen. The three most remembered by the Jordan Crew were Yasuo Kobayashi, Toyokazu Himada and Kennichi Yanagizawa.

Yasuo Kobayashi had studied at the University of Ohio before returning to Japan to fight against the US. He was quite short in stature and for that reason was nicknamed 'Shorty' by the POWs. Kobayashi was a civilian staff member but he had free reign in the cells and was well-known for his brutality. With the help of the guards Kobayashi would frequently enter cells to kick and beat certain men, often Southerners, and especially those who were either shy or seriously wounded.[7] One former POW who was imprisoned with the Jordan Crew, Robert Michelson, provides a typical account concerning Kobayashi.

> Shorty, I believe, was a sadist, because…everything he did was to injure, and to hurt. If you were wounded, and you were in his interrogating room,

that is where they'd put the pressure, on your wounds. And sometimes they were very painful. We had one prisoner, his name was Bob Ring, who was injured from his hip to his knee, a really deep, deep wound. And Bob told us, instead of beating on him, they would just put their sticks inside the wound and twist and twist and twist.[8]

McGraw became a frequent target of Kobayashi's daily beating sessions and, to his dying day, was never able to forget the humiliating abuse that he endured.[9] Kobayashi frequently wandered screaming among the cells to remind prisoners that a death sentence awaited all of them for their part in killing women and children during the Tokyo Firebombings. Whether it was today, tomorrow, or the next day, very soon, the executioners would come for them.[10]

Corporal Toyokazu Himada was a second generation Canadian who also had returned to Japan to join the Imperial Army. His knowledge of current events and American culture both impressed and intimidated Dickerson. Himada served as Kobayashi's right hand man and was present during most interrogation beatings. On numerous occasions, when sick and dying cellmates were being tortured, Himada would watch on and laugh.[11]

Warrant Officer Kennichi Yanagizawa, nicknamed 'Junior' by the prisoners because of his youth and inexperience, had studied in Los Angeles before the war. He spoke better English than Kobayashi. In contrast to Kobayashi and Himada, Yanagizawa was more relaxed and, at times, quite sociable when he was alone with prisoners. Yanagizawa's friendliness had its limits, however. During interrogations he made no moves to restrain guards from beating prisoners while he continued to ask questions. From his facial expressions prisoners knew that Yanagizawa disapproved of what was happening, and he flashed expressions of sympathetic pain and pity as he watched them endure repeated blows from bats and clubs.[12] Grant remembers being escorted by Yanagizawa to his first interrogation. Speaking in a quiet voice full of dejected compassion he whispered to Grant that his interrogators would already know the answer to every question they asked. It would be simpler to just go ahead and give forthright answers.[13] Burkle also remembered his experiences with Yanagizawa kindly.[14]

Prison Facilities

The Main Headquarters of the *kempei-tai* had four stories. The top floor contained the offices for all *kempei-tai* postings throughout the Empire. Administrative offices for the Tokyo area were on the third floor. All of the interrogation chambers were on the second floor. Originally there were only a few temporary holding cells but more were created in a courtyard behind the building and in the basement. These were insufficient for the growing number of downed fliers that were being transferred into their custody, and the conditions were dangerously-overcrowded and unsanitary.[15]

The basement held the 'pig boxes' (*buta bako*) – small cells that measured about three by one and a half meters each. The doors were thick wooden lattices that were secured with huge antiquated padlocks that appeared as if they had come from a Hollywood set. Nine men were crammed into each of these cells. The inmates were a mixture of B-29 crewmen and Japanese political prisoners. Except for one light bulb that burned twenty-four hours a day in the corridor separating the two cellblocks, these cells were continually shrouded in gloom.

The Jordan Crew were split up and kept in the courtyard cells that had been converted from horse stalls. The front of the cells faced an interior corridor where horses had once been led outside to the enclosed courtyard. The other end of this corridor led further inside to the first floor of the Headquarters. The horse stall cells were raised slightly above ground. Pigs and chickens were kept in the courtyard and the prisoners could hear the pigs rooting around below their cells. These cells were larger than the pig boxes (2.5 x 3 x 2.5 meters) and between sixteen to nineteen men could be incarcerated there. One small window was at the ceiling level, which was covered with a heavy black cloth. One light bulb hung from a wire high above. As in the basement cells, this light was never extinguished. Horse stall cells contained mostly B-29 crewmen, though sometimes a Japanese clergyman, Korean agitator, yakuza mobster or a political prisoner would be put in these cells for temporary holding. These inmates were beaten and abused just as much as the Allied POWs.[16]

In the Tower of Hunger

The survivors of the Jordan Crew did not want to speak of their days in these horse stall cells. Most of what was learned came from earlier affidavits that they provided to war crimes investigators or from their private memoirs. Their recorded experiences were corroborated by materials collected from other POWs who were imprisoned at the same time as Jordan and his crew. What follows is only a sample of the horrors that they endured.

Each morning the prisoners would be awakened by the harsh voice of a guard. They would fold their thin, grubby blankets, which were their only personal possessions, in absolute silence. Prisoners were not allowed to speak to each other, though some would risk whispering furtively when the guards' backs were turned. Depending upon the mood of the guards, prisoners would then be blindfolded and forced to sit with their legs folded underneath them for several hours or, in scenes reminiscent of the Abu Ghraib prison more than 60 years later, POWs would be shackled, blindfolded and forced to stand with their arms held outward for long periods. On the days they were allowed to sit as best as they could on the rough, hardwood floors without being blindfolded, the prisoners closest to the cage-like doors of the cells would be kicked constantly by the passing guards.[17]

No prisoner was allowed to shave or take a shower. The cells were infested with lice and other vermin and soon the sweaty, dirty bodies of the Jordan Crew were, together with their cellmates, covered with running sores. Owing to the conditions all the prisoners had severe cases of dysentery. They relieved themselves over a hole in the floor, under which contained a box that collected the waste. Because of the crowded conditions, the floor was frequently covered with the feces of those who could not reach the hole in time.[18]

Two or three times a day a soldier would come and toss tangerine-sized balls of rice onto the filthy floor of the cells. All would drink from the same cup, which the guard would shove through the grating of the cell door to one prisoner at a time. Each was allowed only one cup of water with their rice ball. If anyone spoke or displeased the guards, all of the prisoners in that cell would receive only one rice ball and one cup of water for that day.[19]

There was often a quiet scramble for any rice ball that appeared slightly larger than the others. Trump made an effort not to deprive any who had been imprisoned longer than he, since they all showed signs of advanced starvation.

> There was the young man from Ohio who always wanted my rice ball. We passed them around the circle. If I had brown rice and he had white he wanted brown. If we both had the same, my ball was larger and so I just reached over and exchanged. At home for a number of years he remembered my courtesy and sent me a Christmas card.[20]

Some prisoners invented other ways to get extra food. One man in the cell next to Trump would entertain guards by making bird calls. They would toss him a few scraps as a treat. He would never share his bounty with others in the cell, some of whom were from his own crew.[21] Another way to get extra food was to be chosen for the latrine detail, called *benjo sōji* in Japanese. These 'honey boxes' were carried out to a dumping spot in the courtyard, where the contents would then be used as fertilizer. It was one of the few times that a prisoner could leave his cell.

Sometime in the late morning or early afternoon, a guard would come and inspect the prisoners. Those who had been imprisoned longer knew it was time for the latrine detail and they would whine in high-pitched voices that sounded to Trump like alley cats. In primitive Japanese they would intone, '*benjo sojee, benjo sojee, kino, kino, kino...no benjo sojee.*' This was understood as 'for several days, I haven't been chosen for latrine duty.' Trump found the whole scene degrading and said nothing as the guard walked by. Perhaps because Trump appeared to be so detached he was chosen several times for the task. In the early days, Trump was still strong enough to carry the boxes by himself but he learned very quickly from the malevolent stares of his cellmates that someone should always be asked to 'help' in order that more than one person could get a chance to see the sky and breathe fresh air.

Trump and a cellmate would be tied to a long leash and a guard would escort them (at a respectable distance given what they were carrying) to the collection site at the far end of the courtyard. Along the way they would pass the pig pen, where a slop of rice husks and other unmentionable items lay in a trough. The guard would allow Trump to stop and briefly sink his hand deep into the slop. Trump thought of the story of the prodigal son from the Bible. He had to lean over and would almost always end up spilling the diseased human excrement on what he was able to take from the pigs. He would eat it anyway, calling his special meal 'rice with gravy'.[22]

Some prisoners who were brought in after the Jordan Crew had serious injuries that had been incurred during their capture. Their status as Special Prisoners, and the lack of pharmaceuticals as a result of Operation Starvation, meant that none received any medical treatment. Trump and Burkle both remember one P-51 pilot by the name of Theodore Fox who was thrown into the cell next to theirs. Fox was badly burned, bleeding, and became delirious after a couple of days. They, along with other prisoners, begged the passing guards for help, but the guards would either laugh or ignore them altogether.[23]

As day slipped into night, the guards would order prisoners to prepare to sleep. Everyone would spend about half an hour searching for lice in their blood-stained clothing and hoped they could fall asleep before the lice began biting again. Then they would start the unsightly ritual of laying their stinking bodies firmly next to each other, side-by-side in a manner similar to the historical sketches of African slaves as they were imported to America on ships. One prisoner would always have to sleep by wrapping himself around the fetid hole of the latrine box. Those with long beards would often wake up to find their faces drenched in the contaminated contents of the toilet.[24]

A few nights after they had arrived, the Jordan Crew could not sleep. Fox's condition had grown worse. He started to cry alone in the night and then began to scream. These dying screams continue to this day to haunt the nightmares of the Jordan Crew. Eventually, a guard ran to the cell and began to beat Fox for breaking the rule of silence. Burkle watched through a crack in the cell wall as the guard beat Fox so badly that his abdomen split and part of an intestine became exposed.[25] Early the next morning, Fox, now comatose, was dragged from the cell. Robert Michelson recalls what happened next.

> But then for one of the men that was wounded, he was taken out of the cell, laid on his back in the hallway, and somebody came by and injected something with a syringe, and he died…and he was placed on a pile of dung, of horse shit. It stayed there for about three days, and then it disappeared. The reason we know this is that we were in the number one cell and could just glance outside that door. So that's what the Japanese think of Americans—they're horse shit.[26]

Internal Hell

As they sat in the overcrowded cells on the Japanese version of bread and water the Jordan Crew began to fantasize about food. Grant recalls that he constantly thought about the weekly supply of whisky that his father, who owned a liquor store, would send to him on Tinian. He wondered who was enjoying his whisky now.[27] Trump was mentally tortured by an Italian prisoner next to him who would whisper his favorite recipes. 'Just the thing for hunger pains,' he remarked.

> I believe thirst was a bigger problem for me in the month of July. I could envision the milk pitcher in our refrigerator at home or the old coca cola

cooler at the fire hall. I vividly recalled the image of the No. 10 can of turkey in the bomb bay and made up my mind that the next time we were shot down, we would eat lunch before the target.[28]

When Trump was a boy, he often rebelled against the Christian faith of his father – something which is common among the sons of ministers. His father, however, had devised clever ways of bribing him into reading the Bible and attending church. Trump now appreciated what his father had done for him. While he was in the cells Trump would meditate on the liturgy and scriptures, resigning himself into the Hands of the Lord. He wanted to share his faith and some words of hope with others, but also didn't want to risk the severe beating from guards if they caught him speaking. This decision to remain silent became a source of great pain and regret for the rest of his life.[29]

His shame was unnecessary. The mental state of most of Trump's cellmates had deteriorated to the point that they were neither willing nor able to hear the Good News he had to share.

> To be honest with you, you're starving, and you're hurting. And when I say starving, I don't just mean you're hungry. Your gums begin to bleed, and your legs are swelling up, and your beard is growing—it's full of shit anyway, because your beard is floating in that box of *banjo-soje* [latrine box] —and you're weak. You couldn't stand if you wanted to. Your condition is such that you, you withdraw. Your mind will not even think about what is happening, and so you just withdraw from everything, and you try to become a blank. You're nothing. In your own mind, you do not dare think about anything. I think your mind is trying to save you, because you'd go nuts. So you just withdraw, and you exist, but beyond existence, there's nothing.[30]

The prisoners burned with silent hate towards their captors, and Yasuo Kobayashi in particular. Their fantasies of vengeance caused them to sink further into a downward spiral that sapped their strength and damaged their minds.

> We no longer talked – we just sat or stood and stared at nothing. I felt nothing. Our hatred of the Japanese military, the Japanese culture, the Japanese inhumanity, cranked up notch after notch. How many more notches could our hatred go? This intense hatred built up in me until sometimes I thought I would choke. About all we could do was pray and hope that God heard us. We prayed and prayed to our Almighty God for help. I worried that God would not hear me through such hate. I tried to overcome it. I really tried. Once I even tried praying for Shorty, but I wasn't sincere. I doubt that I helped him anyway.[31]

The hatred and resentment resulting from their maltreatment was only amplified by the racism endemic in blue collar America at the time. Army Air Force indoctrination and American war propaganda played on what today would be seen as shockingly racist portrayals of the Japanese as devious, sub-human, and vicious.[32] The fact that African Americans were not allowed to serve on B-29s is also evocative of the level of racial discrimination that plagued the US military. Now the tables had been turned. Yasuo Kobayashi was free to live out the dark dreams of discriminated minorities everywhere by wielding total power over those who had been the symbols of his own oppression when he lived in the United States. The Caucasian men tortured by Kobayashi received a hell-like lesson in what it was like to be an oppressed minority. However, nothing had changed in this transaction. Kobayashi had become the very type of person he despised and his wards only learned to hate the Japanese even more as they suffered the ignominy of being forced to endure beatings from one who was, in their estimation, inferior. This racism, compounded by starvation and physical abuse, did not allow them to recognize that the Japanese prisoners who shared their cells also shared equally in the suffering.

The POWs were also unaware that many of the Japanese soldiers also hated their superiors just as much as they did for the beatings and humiliation that they endured daily. Tameichi Hara, a Captain of a Japanese destroyer, remembers that, 'Certain of my seniors were sadistic brutes. They took singular delight in terrorizing freshmen. To this day I feel a revulsion at seeing these men...'[33]

Fighter pilot Saburo Sakai wrote after the war, '...never, while I was in training or later, has my deep-rooted anger at the brutality of the petty officers abated.'[34]

Another soldier described his experience thus: 'The first day we joined, everyone spoke to us kindly and treated us gently, as if we were guests. But then on the second day, oh, then the beatings began.'[35]

Hatred burned in the hearts of many Japanese soldiers towards their superiors, but their beatings were so frequent and severe that after a short time most lacked the will to resist. Hara explains, 'After a few months of such treatment [we] became sheeplike in [our] obedience. Every man's face bore evidence of the brutality we endured.'[36] Brutality begets brutality, and the Jordan Crew would have to endure further experiences of such cruelty during the only other time they left their cells – the interrogation sessions.

Interrogation Experiences

The officer in charge of interrogation at the Tokyo Headquarters, Lt. Toshio Toyama, had drawn up a list of instructions on how staff and interrogators were to deal with the prisoners. These instructions included the following:

- Since Japan has not signed the Hague Pact, it is permissible to beat prisoners.
- Take a strict attitude and show no mildness to the prisoners.
- If the prisoners withhold information or deliberately falsify information, beat them but fulfill your duties as police investigators.
- It is not much use to hit American fliers in the face because they are all adept at boxing. Slapping is supposed to have more effect than a punch.

- Beat them on the back with a bamboo fencing stick.
- Do not allow prisoners to sit on a chair; have them kneel Japanese style. That should make interrogation more effective.[37]

At this stage in the war, however, some interrogators had become far more permissive and friendly in their demeanor, leading some to believe they were trying to curry favor with POWs in an effort to avoid retaliation after the war.[38] The way each member of Jordan's crew was treated during their interrogations differed significantly. Interrogations were an almost daily occurrence and followed the same bewildering patterns that the Jordan Crew had experienced in Niigata. The interrogators would normally ask questions regarding their feelings towards the war, technical aspects of the B-29, or about their family back at home. The manner in which each man was treated during interrogations varied partly as a result of how they reacted to their captors. Those who showed a calm or sincere attitude were treated with a modicum of decency, but those who revealed feelings of contempt or displeasure would be beaten with sword-like wooden fencing sticks (*shinai*).[39]

Most of the interrogators had been exchange students studying in California just before the war broke out. Some had been drafted while visiting their families in Japan and they made it clear to members of the Jordan Crew that they felt just as much as if they were prisoners of the Japanese army. Burkle remembered that some of these former students had been quite decent to him. He reported that, apart from the appalling conditions in the cells, he was personally never physically abused, except for being required to stand with his hands above his head for several hours, something he saw as childish.[40] Burkle's interrogators seemed to be primarily interested in the Japanese balloon bomb campaign that took place in late 1944 to early 1945, in which balloons carrying incendiary bombs and antipersonnel mines had been sent over the Pacific with the hope of wreaking havoc in American cities.

Trump also recalled that, while he never received medical attention for the wounds inflicted on him by the villagers near Kyōgase, he was only very rarely struck or threatened during interrogations.[41] However, Trump's interrogations took an unexpected turn later, which ultimately and inadvertently put him at odds with his fellow prisoners.

Trump's youth, expressiveness and well-mannered demeanor brought him to the attention of a high-ranking officer in the headquarters. Trump was educated and articulate; the officer seemed to take great interest in speaking with him about various social problems in the United States. In subsequent interrogations Trump was taken to a small room, given a pen and paper, and told to write essays about some of America's problems, such as youth delinquency. This request struck Trump as being rather an odd and futile piece of busywork, but since the *kempei-tai* rarely if ever took no for an answer, and as it was a welcome respite from the overcrowded, squalid cell, he complied. They left him there for hours and frequently forgot to give him a rice ball for lunch.[42] The men in his cell began to watch these developments with growing suspicion. The latrine details were too frequent, and he was gone far longer than the others for interrogations. Part of the suspicion stemmed from the experience of others who had also been approached by a ranking Japanese officer.

> The next morning I was again taken before the same senior officer. He dismissed the guards and 'invited' me to sit down. He appeared overly friendly. Why? I was subjected to another full day of questions. The same questions as before, the same answers as before. Then he branched off into a discussion centered around American feelings about the war and Japan's will to win a settlement for an honorable peace or fight to the last Japanese life when the Americans invaded. He said that Japanese culture dictated that death was better than a disgraceful peace. I didn't understand what he was telling me and was puzzled why we were having this 'buddy-buddy' discussion.
>
> I really came to attention at his next statement. He told me that my relatives would not know that I'd survived and would never be notified so long as I was a Special Prisoner. 'But,' he said, 'your status could be changed.' He went on to say, very confidentially, and in a low, soft voice, that many prisoners volunteered to broadcast messages to America...My head jerked back and I stared at him. He continued, 'Would you be interested in letting your family know you are alive and being treated well in a better prison than this one, in a camp where you would have medical treatment and good food?' I said, 'Yes, I would like for my parents to know that I am alive. Yes, I want very much to be transferred to a regular POW camp.' He knew that I knew exactly what he was offering and would not be of value to the Japanese propaganda program. His whole countenance changed. He frowned. He closed his interrogation log. The matter ended that instant.[43]

The experience of others on the crew was very different from that of Trump and Burkle. Jordan continued to maintain his sober, austere deportment, which had served him well in Niigata. But now in Tokyo he came across as arrogant and stubborn. According to Jordan, during the twenty-eight days of his captivity, he was interrogated a total of twenty-four times, and four times he was interrogated all night. To soften him up, Jordan was frequently forced to lay face down on a hard concrete floor while his interrogator, an officer fitting the description of Lt. Toyama, would walk up and down his spine with riding boots. When the officer wished to emphasize a certain point, he would jump up and down on Jordan's buttocks, or stand on his head, crushing his face further into the concrete.[44] McGraw received similar treatment, being constantly questioned about the technical aspects of the B-29. The interrogators believed that, as a Master Sergeant, he would be privy to valuable technological secrets. When McGraw failed to meet their expectations, he was tied to a chair and beaten for long periods of time by Yasuo Kobayashi.[45]

Some interrogations were obviously designed to break the men psychologically. Grant and Dickerson both remembered how each had been brought to a chamber where the interrogator, Corporal Toyokazu Himada, waited calmly at a table. On top of the table lay an American .45 automatic. Himada would order the crewman to sit opposite and disassemble the weapon. This they would do. Then the interrogator would tell him to put the weapon back together again. At this point, the soldier would begin to wonder if he was assembling the instrument of his own execution.[46] Dickerson either couldn't or wouldn't put the weapon back together again. For this, he was severely beaten.[47]

Leading Questions

Recently discovered historical documents have suggested that the Japanese military either knew or suspected that the United States was developing an atomic bomb, based on what they learned from German intelligence and from their own efforts to create such a weapon. The reason why the *kempei-tai* asked the same questions repeatedly was to lull the prisoners into a daze, and then they would slip in key questions related to intelligence they wished to gather. From the scraps of stories pieced together from different B-29 crewmen it seems clear that, even before the first atomic bomb had been dropped on Hiroshima, the *kempei-tai* was aware that something was afoot. Their questions often focused on learning anything about the 509th stationed on Tinian or of B-29s that had been modified in some way. Michelson remembers one interrogation session.

> Their main questions were, 'Have you ever seen a B-29 with only one bomb bay?' The answer was of course no—they had two. So one would be unusual. 'Have I ever seen a bomb bay door that has been modified?' No. 'Have I ever seen a bomb bay that's been modified?' No. 'What's the biggest bomb you could carry?' And I said, 'Ten or twelve thousand pounds of bombs, depending on the gas load or the target.' 'What's the biggest bomb I have ever seen?' And I said, 'I haven't seen anything bigger than what we carry, but I have heard of one called the blockbuster, used in England, and it decimates a large area when it hits the ground.' Not until after the war did I realize that they were saying that, if you carry an atomic bomb in a B-29, you have to modify the bomb bay and the bomb bay door. Of course I didn't know that, but it was after the war I realized the import of their question.[48]

During his first interrogation, Trump was knocked out of his chair for failing to mention the 509th, the subject to which the interrogators returned in subsequent sessions. Before they had been shot down, Trump had heard such rumors from another airman by the name of Wagner, who was a navigator on a plane that flew supply and transport missions for the 509th out of California, Utah and New Mexico. Trump related the following story to his interrogators.

> He [Wagner] came to my barracks, and he told me, he said, 'We're gonna win the war with one plane.' I said, 'you can't be kidding me…there's nothing up there to bomb down there anymore. It's all burnt down. Tokyo's flat. I don't know what you're talking about. How are you gonna end the war?' He wouldn't tell me, but he said, 'You just wait. We're gonna win the war.'[49]

There was nothing disloyal in providing this information, since Trump and others on the Jordan Crew had been advised during intelligence briefings that if captured, with the exception of radar frequencies for air sea rescue, they could tell their interrogators anything they knew, and even exaggerate if they thought the misinformation would demoralize the enemy. It wasn't until later that Trump realized that his friend had been referring to the A-bomb. Grant had remarked that everyone on Tinian knew that the Enola Gay carried some sort of secret weapon, since no one was allowed near the plane.[50] This might be one of the reasons why Jordan's interrogations were particularly long and brutal. The Jordan Crew's plane was only a few hardstands away from the Enola Gay and other planes in the 509th.[51] Being the captain of a plane parked so close to the 509th, perhaps the *kempei-tai* believed that he was privy to classified information. In the final analysis, however, it was their reliance upon torture and intimidation in intelligence gathering that would prove to be the *kempei-tai's* undoing.

The McDilda Affair and the Jordan Crew

On August 6, 1945, the first A-bomb was dropped on Hiroshima. Even before Truman's official radio announcement, Allied code breakers intercepted a Japanese naval message reporting Hiroshima had been destroyed by an atomic bomb (*genshi bakudan*), lending credence to the belief that elements within Japan's intelligence community had been aware of America's A-Bomb development.[52] Historians Jim Smith and Malcolm McConnell have woven together the research of a number of earlier historians about a little-known but significant incident that took place soon after the attack on Hiroshima.[53] It concerns the capture of P-51 fighter pilot Marcus McDilda and his role in Japan's decision to surrender. What was unknown until now is that members of the Jordan Crew were also involved in this episode.

Lt. McDilda had been shot down on August 8 near Osaka. He was fished out of the bay where he had been floating for several hours on his life raft, and then he was beaten by angry civilians. Now he was tied to a chair in the Osaka Headquarters, and was proving to be unresponsive to the interrogators' standard methods of brutal persuasion.

The *kempei-tai* officers wanted McDilda to tell them everything he knew about the A-bomb. He stated that he didn't know anything more than what he had heard on the radio. A Japanese general who was observing the interrogation then drew his sword, walked up to McDilda, and slowly sliced open his bottom lip. He told McDilda that if he did not start telling everything he knew about the atomic bomb, he would personally cut off his head.

McDilda was inclined to believe the general, and in what must surely be one of the most dramatic examples of quick thinking under pressure, he began to spin a cunning tale. He told the interrogators how the US had developed a huge bomb that was covered in a lead shield. Inside were two containers charged with positive and negative energies. When the bomb was dropped, the lead shield melted, releasing the opposing forces to create a bolt of lightning that was so powerful, it could flatten an entire city.

The interrogators feverishly took notes. McDilda's tale seemed to account for the reports they had received from survivors of a huge flash just before the explosion. They now asked McDilda about the next targets. He told them that Tokyo was scheduled to be bombed in the next few days.

The interrogators were convinced. A message was sent immediately to Tokyo and terror gripped the Imperial Palace. The military had already considered this possibility, and now McDilda's story confirmed their worst fears. If there was a risk to the Emperor, it was vital to get him and the Imperial Family out of Tokyo immediately. Historian Richard Frank writes that they began to urgently look for ways to escape Tokyo quickly.[54]

On the morning of August 9, at the same time that McDilda had been brought to Tokyo, Trump and Jordan were summoned to what they thought would be another interrogation. Instead they were given a shave and a bath with a cold hose, which was very refreshing in the hot August weather. They were fed a lunch that included fish heads and tails and then were clothed in new American uniforms. Now that they were presentable, they were taken to a room where they were seated, from the manner in which the guards and officers acted in his presence, in front of a very high-ranking Japanese official.

The official spoke excellent English and, after a couple of hours of questioning, it became apparent to Trump that the war was nearly over. Trump was asked whether, if Gordon piloted a plane, he could navigate without the benefit of radio or radar. Trump replied that he could, and the official told him that there would be a chance that he and Jordan would transport some VIPs to an undisclosed location. Trump was excited, thinking maybe they would be flying Japanese officials to surrender to the Allied forces. This would be history in the making, and he said that he would cooperate.

At the same time that Trump and Jordan were being briefed, nearby at the Prime Minister's air-raid shelter, a frantic meeting had been called. The main topic of discussion was the USSR's declaration of war, which had been accompanied by their invasion of Manchuria. Members of the military high command who were present ignored this, focusing instead on repelling the anticipated American invasion. They voiced confidence that the Allies could still be brought to a negotiated truce through the threat of inflicting large numbers of casualties on the invaders. But the peace faction, armed with McDilda's misinformation that an atomic bomb might soon be dropped on Tokyo, urged for an immediate and unconditional surrender.[55]

Before Trump and Jordan were returned to their cells, the Japanese official closed his notebook and asked Trump what he planned on doing after the war. Trump said that he wanted to go back to college and study to be a Christian minister. The man was moved by the words and, with genuine warmth, extended his hand to Trump, who took it into his and shook it. The official wished him well and for Trump's part, this was the moment when he began to love his enemies.[56]

In a nearby interrogation chamber, McDilda was being pressed for technical data on the Bomb. He eventually broke down and admitted that he didn't know anything and that his whole story had been a fabrication. He was beaten and thrown in the basement pig box cells; Trump and Jordan remained in theirs.[57]

Trump's return was too much for the prisoners in his cell. They had had plenty of time to ruminate over his numerous chances to leave for latrine duty, the interrogations that lasted far longer than anyone else's, and now he showed up showered, shaved and in clean clothes. Dickerson reported that whispered rumors began to spread from cell to cell that Trump was being prepared for propaganda broadcasts.[58] Memories of this unfounded rumor still evoked strong emotions in surviving members of the Jordan Crew today, and it forever cast a 'cloud of unknowing' between Trump and the rest of the Crew.[59] It is a mystery as to why Jordan was never implicated in this rumor, and also why Jordan makes no mention of any of these events in his affidavit.

Many today would like to believe that despite the starvation, lice, beatings, torture, mind-numbing hatred and groans of dying men tearing at what strings of compassion were left in their hearts, humanity would still somehow triumph in the prison of the *kempei-tai*. It did not. Jealousy for an extra grain of rice created animosity that lasted a lifetime. Special treatment of any kind would evoke cruel malice. Even without these factors, it is easiest to believe the worst about newcomers. For Trump, at the very moment he began to live out Christ's command as best he could in the most difficult of circumstances, was falsely accused by his fellow prisoners. Such is the nature of things in dark places, where starving young men are finally reduced to consuming themselves in hatred.

A few hours after McDilda's admission, Nagasaki was bombed. The prisoners in Tokyo were unaware of what had happened, but there was a dark intensity from the guards that frightened the prisoners. Yasuo Kobayashi began to rant incoherently in the cellblocks. Some unknown menace was in the works. Downing's interviews with Lt. Col. Ranjo Fujino at the Tokyo Headquarters after the war found that the commanding officers at this time were considering drastic measures:

> I interrogated him and asked him if anyone had made any plans to execute the American fliers at the end of the war, and he said, 'Yes, Col. Otani spoke to me on about 9 August…and then again on 14 August and suggested to me that the fliers should be executed. He explained to me that Japan had lost the war and that if the American fliers were liberated and permitted to return home, they would tell how they were treated in the Tokyo Kempei Tai headquarters.'[60]

Saner minds eventually prevailed in Tokyo, but not in Osaka. Over fifty American fliers were beheaded by the *kempei-tai* in retaliation for Nagasaki.[61] McDilda's ruse had demoralized the enemy and saved his life. Five days later the Jordan Crew, together with McDilda and the rest of the Allied POWs held in the Tokyo Headquarters, were rousted from their cells and told to get ready to leave.

[1] Scott Downing, *The Horse Stalls at Kempei Tai*, in *The Global Twentieth: An Anthology of the 20th Air Force in World War II (Volume 1)*, ed. Marshall, Chester (Memphis: Marshall Publishers), 193.

[2] Scott Downing, 194.

[3] Kenji Hall, 'Japan's A-Bomb Goal Still Long Way Off in '45,' *The Japan Times*, March 7 2003, http://www.japantimes.com/cgi-bin/makeprfy.pl5?nn20030307b7.htm. (accessed September 19, 2005). Deborah Shapley, 'Nuclear Weapons History: Japan's Wartime Bomb Projects Revealed,' *Science* 199, no. 4325 (January 13, 1978): 152-157. Haruko Taya Cook and Theodore F. Cook, *Japan at War: An Oral History* (New York: The New Press, 2000), 119-202.

[4] Louis Allen, 'Japanese Intelligence Systems,' *Journal of Contemporary History* 22, no. 4 (October 1987), 553-554.

[5] Yukio Sugano, interview by Toshihide Uemura, July 3, 1998, tape recording, The B-29 Downing Incident (B29 撃墜事件について), Former Yokogōshi City History Department, Yokogōshi, Niigata.

[6] Robert Burkle, 'Affidavit' (Judge Advocate General (Army), Record Group 153, War Crimes Branch Case Files, Case 35-1305, 1944-1949, photocopied).

[7] Robert Grant, interview by author, October 25, 2005, MD Recording.

[8] Robert Michelson, interview by Thomas Saylor (Apple Valley, Minnesota, November 2, 2001), *Prisoner of War Oral History Project: World War Two and Korea* (2001-2002), http://people.csp.edu/saylor/POWproject/POWinterviews/MichelsonR.htm. (accessed February 7, 2006).

[9] William Conine, e-mail message to author, March 5, 2005.

[10] Fiske Hanley, *Accused American War Criminal* (Austin, TX: Eakin Press, 1997), 115-116.

[11] Dickerson called his torturer 'Toyokazu Hikida', while Fiske Hanley cites war crimes documents that name him as Toyokazu Himada. As cited in Walter Dickerson, Champaign County, Illinois, Affidavit to War Crimes Office, Civil Affairs Division, October 16, 1947, Private Papers of Robert Neptune, Fiske Hanley Collection, Ft. Worth, Texas.

[12] Fiske Hanley, 115. Robert Michelson, November 2, 2001.

[13] Robert Grant, interview by author, April 23, 2004, MD Recording.

[14] Robert Burkle, 'Affidavit,' Case 35-1305.

[15] Scott Downing, 193, 195.

[16] Robert Grant, October 25, 2005. Paul Trump, 'War Memories,' 2003, unpublished manuscript (photocopy), 1, Trump Family Papers, Lititz, PA.

[17] Robert Burkle, 'Affidavit,' Case 35-1305. Robert Burkle, 'Affidavit' (Judge Advocate General (Army), Record Group 153, War Crimes Branch Case Files, Case 33-130, 1944-1949, photocopied).

[18] Robert Michelson, November 2, 2001.

[19] Robert Burkle, 'Affidavit,' Case 33-130. Scott Downing, 189-191.

[20] Paul Trump, 'War Memories,' 5.

[21] Paul Trump, 'War Memories,' 4.

[22] Paul Trump, 'War Memories,' 5. Paul Trump, interview by author, September 13, 2004, MD Recording. Paul Trump, interview by author, March 23, 2004, MD Recording.

[23] Robert Burkle, 'Affidavit,' Case 35-1305. Paul Trump, Phoenixville, Pennsylvania, Affidavit to War Crimes Office, Judge Advocate's Office, October 30, 1947, Private Papers of Robert Neptune, Fiske Hanley Collection, Ft. Worth, Texas.

[24] Paul Trump, 'War Memories,' 4. Robert Michelson, November 2, 2001.

[25] Robert Burkle, 'Affidavit,' Case 35-1305. Robert Burkle, 'Affidavit,' Case 33-130. Paul Trump, October 30, 1947.

[26] Robert Michelson, November 2, 2001.

[27] Robert Grant, April 23, 2004.

[28] Paul Trump, 'War Memories,' 5.

[29] Paul Trump, 'War Memories,' 5.

[30] Robert Michelson, November 2, 2001.

[31] Fiske Hanley, 165.

[32] Even more virulent posters and films prevalent during this era, such as the *Tokio Kid* series, depicted gross caricatures of Japanese torturing and murdering Caucasian women.

[33] Tameichi Hara, Fred Saito, and Roger Pineau, *Japanese Destroyer Captain* (New York: Ballentine Books, 1961), 15.

[34] Saburo Sakai, Martin Caidin, and Fred Saito, *Samurai!* (New York: Ballentine Books, 1958), 19.

[35] Yuichi Hatto, interview by author, February 22, 2005, Tokyo, MD Recording.

[36] Tameichi Hara, Fred Saito, and Roger Pineau, 16.

[37] Scott Downing, 194.

[38] Raymond 'Hap' Halloran, e-mail message to author, February 8, 2006.

[39] Technically, *shinai* are not clubs, but wooden replicas of Samurai swords that are used in Kendo training.

[40] Robert Burkle, 'Affidavit,' Case 33-130.

[41] Paul Trump, October 30, 1947.

[42] Paul Trump, 'War Memories,' 5. Paul Trump, September 13, 2004. Paul Trump, March 23, 2004.

[43] Fiske Hanley, 132-133.

[44] As he made notes for his own book, Fiske Hanley wrote on his copies of official affidavits obtained from Robert Neptune, a defense attorney for Japanese who had been accused of war crimes. Besides Jordan's description of the officer who tortured him, Hanley wrote the name 'Toyama'. Hanley had also endured brutal interrogations from Toyama during his incarceration at the Kempei-tai Headquarters. As cited in Gordon P. Jordan, Miami Beach, Florida, Affidavit, Legal Section (GHQ SCAP), December 4, 1945, Private Papers of Robert Neptune, Fiske Hanley Collection, Ft. Worth, Texas.

[45] Benny Doyle Conine Sr. and William Doswell Conine, III, 'Conine Brothers' Early Years,' 2005, unpublished manuscript (photocopy), p. 270, Family Memoirs, The Woodlands, Texas.

[46] Robert Grant, April 23, 2004.

[47] Walter Dickerson, October 16, 1947.

[48] Robert Michelson, November 2, 2001.

[49] Paul Trump, March 23, 2004. Paul Trump, September 13, 2004.

[50] Robert Grant, e-mail message to author, November 2, 2005.

[51] Paul Trump, March 23, 2004.

[52] Michael Smith, *The Emperor's Codes* (New York: Bantam Press, 2001), 274.

[53] Jim B. Smith and Malcolm McConnell, *The Last Mission: The Secret Story of World War II's Final Battle* (New York: Broadway Books, 2003), 111-113.

[54] Richard B. Frank, *Downfall: The End of the Japanese Imperial Empire* (New York: Penguin Books, 2001), 269-270.

[55] Jim B. Smith and Malcolm McConnell, 113-114.

[56] Paul Trump, 'War Memories,' 5. Paul Trump, September 13, 2004. Paul Trump, March 23, 2004.

[57] Paul Trump, 'War Memories,' 5. Fiske Hanley, 246.

[58] Walter Dickerson, October 16, 1947.

[59] Robert Grant, interview by author, November 27, 2005, Digital Recording.

[60] Scott Downing, 195.

[61] Fiske Hanley, 166-67, 246.

CHAPTER TEN

TO ŌMORI AND HOME

On August 15 the survivors of the Jordan Crew were blindfolded and put into dirty, wood-burning trucks. They sat with other prisoners as they rumbled their way towards Tokyo Harbor. There they stopped, and everyone was brought to the water's edge and told to kneel. As they waited on the shore, some wondered if they were going to be executed. Then the blindfolds were removed. They were told to strip and wash themselves in the ocean. This was the first time for most of the crew to take a bath in nearly a month, and it had been much longer for other prisoners. They laughed like boys again as they splashed in the water. Some, however, looked back at the shore to see a disturbing scene.

> I don't know how long I was in the water, but I turned around and looked from where we had come on the shore, because we could hear noises back there. Three machine guns had been set up on the shore, and Shorty was directing the machine guns. So I thought, 'Well, we are going to be machine gunned in the water, or as we come out of the water.' And I thought, 'Geez, I can swim, if I can swim under water, I might survive.' But there was a terrific argument at the machine guns between Shorty and Junior, the two interrogators. Shorty issued orders, and he left. And the machine guns were packed up and put in the fourth truck, and that truck drove away, leaving us there with Junior. And Junior said, 'You're going to walk out on a causeway' – which we could now see, I think to the left – 'and on the end of that causeway is a prisoner of war camp. That's where you're going.' And he marched us out to that prisoner of war camp.[1]

As they shuffled into Camp Ōmori, wet and half-naked, they stood at attention to hear speeches from the camp commandant, Col. Kaname Sakaba, and from the ranking American officer among the POWs. Then they were escorted to a barracks that was cordoned off from the rest of the camp.

By sending furtive whispers to each other from the horse stall cells they had already determined that Adams, Hawkins, Spero and Wride were not in their number. But this was the first time for the crew actually to gather and see each other face-to-face since their mission briefing on Tinian several weeks earlier. It was a cheerless reunion. They were exhausted and emaciated from their ordeal. Each slowly recognized the faces of others in the crew. They shuffled together to form a small but morose huddle.[2] No one wanted to talk. Just standing together was about all they could bear for the moment.

Camp Ōmori

The Tokyo Main POW Camp in the ward of Ōmori was created in September 1942. It was thrown together after Japan had acquired an unexpectedly large number of Allied POWs from their conquests of the Philippines, South East Asia and Guam. The camp sat on an artificial island in Tokyo Bay and could only be reached by one connecting wooden bridge. Camp Ōmori became the central headquarters for all other POW camps in the Tokyo area. Several 'sub-camps' and 'dispatch camps' from as far away as Niigata were under the direct administrative authority of the headquarters at Ōmori. Staff and guards were frequently rotated back and forth from the camps in Niigata. Ōmori's location in Tokyo, as well as the fact that it housed the main headquarters, meant that it also became a prime location for propaganda. Red Cross and Vatican officials were frequently funneled to Ōmori to make their inspections.

POW Camp Ōmori in August 1945.
(NARA.)

The conditions at Ōmori were similar to those of other Japanese POW camps on Honshu. The POWs, who consisted of mainly American, British and Dutch soldiers, worked as forced laborers for various shipping companies in and around Tokyo Bay. The American POWs had worked out agreements with a number of staff and Japanese soldiers to share in the bounty of all manner of foodstuffs that they stole during the day. POWs ate far better at Ōmori than those in other camps that were further away from the constant gaze of Tokyo's administration.

The relations between POWs were constantly strained, and divided along old world and new world lines. The British POWs generally looked down on the Americans for stealing food, seeing this as conduct unbecoming to a professional soldier. It was anathema for British soldiers to steal food, since those who suffered were civilians, not enemy soldiers. The Dutch were not above stealing food, but they kept to themselves and would not interact with outsiders unless they needed something. The Americans thought the British were arrogant and far too friendly with the Japanese staff. The few New Zealanders, Australians and Canadian POWs in the camp usually banded with the Americans against the British. As a result, whenever someone was caught by the strict guards in some infraction, it was usually believed that the British soldiers had been the informants.[3]

Camp Staff

The dynamics among the Japanese staff at Ōmori were also very similar to other POW camps in Japan. According to Yuichi Hatto, a clerk who served at Ōmori throughout most of the war, being assigned to a POW camp brought shame and dishonor to a person and his family. Such a posting was reserved for losers and misfits who were of little use to the Army. Serving in a POW camp for a Japanese soldier was akin to the American soldier who had to tell his friends that, instead of fighting on Omaha Beach during the D-Day invasion, he had been assigned to waste disposal duty in a backwater of Louisiana. The effects of bearing this shame in silence took its toll on people in different ways, according to Hatto. The majority approached their duties with ambivalence, paying little attention to the POWs or to anything else. Two other minorities existed. One was a group that befriended the POWs. These were considered pariahs to their fellow Japanese soldiers. The other group resorted to exploiting or abusing the POWs as a means of assuaging their own wounded psyche.

Col. Sakaba was from the same graduating class as General Tōjō. He had graduated at the bottom of the class and, while he was still a Colonel, most of Sakaba's classmates had become generals or were occupying influential posts in the Empire. During drinking bouts with his officers Sakaba often said that, before he died, he wanted to hear himself being addressed as a General. Sakaba significantly increased the labor requirements of all the POWs in his administrative area to demonstrate to his superiors that he was making an important contribution to the war effort, and thereby deserved a promotion. Hatto lamented that one of the unknown tragedies of the war was that thousands of Allied POWs suffered and died in order to satisfy the vanity of one man.[4]

A camp guard that was a constant source of pain to the POWs was Matsuhiro Watanabe, who they nicknamed 'The Bird'. Watanabe came from a very well-to-do family and he struggled with the shame of being assigned to Ōmori. One day he could be friendly and the next, when he became afraid of losing control over the POWs, he would lash out with fearful violence.[5] Grant recalls that soon after his arrival at Ōmori he was able to steal a bit of food but was immediately caught and given a ferocious beating by Watanabe.[6] In anticipation of the vengeance that was to come, the Japanese Office of POW Affairs issued a directive to all camps which allowed personnel who might fear reprisals the chance to flee and go into hiding. Watanabe disappeared from the camp soon afterwards and successfully avoided prosecution from war crimes. Just before his death an elderly Watanabe came forth to try to explain who he was and to apologize for what he did.

> There were two people inside me. One that followed military orders, and another that was human. At times I felt I had a good heart, but Japan at that time had a bad heart. In normal times I would never had done such things.[7]

Even though Ōmori was a very unpleasant place to be, to the Jordan Crew and the others who had been released from the *kempei-tai* headquarters, the camp felt like a country club. Food was plentiful in comparison to what they had in the horse stall cells, and they received the same amount of rations as a Japanese civilian. They could go outside the barracks anytime and officers were paid a Japanese salary according to their equivalent rank in the Japanese army.[8] They began to cheer up a bit as they felt the sun on their faces once more. Members of the crew met and befriended Maj. Greg 'Pappy' Boyington, a navy fighter ace made famous later in the television series 'Baa Baa Black Sheep'. They settled in with tired expectation and learned with everyone else that the war truly was over. Soon they would all return home.

Incidents and Events at Ōmori

The crew stayed at Ōmori for only two weeks, but it was a tumultuous time. Some of this is described in Robert Martindale's *The 13th Mission*. One memory that stayed with the crew was when, a few days after they had arrived, a Japanese soldier who had too much to drink attempted to commit ritual suicide (*seppuku*).

On August 22 Trump and Jordan were asked to sit on an officer's tribunal to decide what to do about certain POWs who had been interned at the nearby Bunka Propaganda Camp, and who had just been transferred to Ōmori. One American sergeant in particular, by the name of John David Provoo, had been accused of aiding the enemy and informing on other prisoners, which had resulted in their deaths. Trump had met Provoo briefly and learned that he had been the son of a Christian missionary and had grown up in Japan. Provoo was fluent in Japanese and had a deeper understanding of Japanese people's thinking than other POWs, but he had still crossed the line. The tribunal found Provoo guilty and ordered that he be kept under arrest in a room somewhere on camp.[9] The other POWs from the Bunka Camp, who had participated in anti-American propaganda broadcasts and, as a reward, had been well-fed on Red Cross parcels, were to be shunned by the rest of those in the camp. Trump remembered feeling some measure of pity for these men, but he avoided contact with them once they had been convicted by the camp tribunal.[10]

Photo taken from a B-29 of Ōmori Camp during a relief mission
to drop food and medicine by parachute.
(Richard Keenan. *The 20th Air Force Album*. Washington, DC: 20th Air Force
Association, 1982, 168.)

B-29 food drops became more frequent. During some of the earlier relief missions the parachutes either did not open or were unable to handle the weight of the steel barrels that contained all manner of food items. Trump remembers wryly how one barrel full of Mounds chocolate bars fell right into the area where the contents of the latrines had just been dumped. The chocolate bars still looked delicious regardless of where they were floating, leaving him feeling rather conflicted as to what to do.[11]

More Information about the Missing Crewmen

The jubilation of the last days in Ōmori helped the Jordan Crew to come out of their shells and start talking to each other once more. They began to speak about what they remembered from the last mission as they tried to piece together what had happened to the men who didn't make it. Everyone agreed that Hawkins had probably decided 'to ride it down' – airmen's slang for willingly going down with one's plane. Based on Grant's recollection, Spero, they surmised, was probably one who fought it out on the ground, and who was subsequently killed. Adams could have done the same. It was a tense situation and he could have lashed out with predictably fatal consequences. They were uncertain about Wride, but based on Trump's memories and what they learned from the *kempei-tai* officers in Niigata, it was possible that he went down with the plane. Except for Dickerson's story of how he was captured, however, no one else had fired their weapons, but almost all remembered hearing at least two other exchanges of weapons fire in the night.

It happened that some of the guards in Ōmori had been transferred in from Niigata 5B. One had been on that night-time hunt for the Jordan Crew. The guard learned that the Jordan Crew was trying to find out what had happened to their comrades.

This guard cautiously approached the crew. He told them that he had been there when one of their crewmen had been killed. According to the guard, this crewman had tried to fight it out with civilians and had wounded three or four of them with his weapon. He had tried to crawl under a small bridge or into a culvert, but he was pulled out and then beheaded. The guard showed them a set of first lieutenant's bars that he had kept as a trophy.[12] Some on the crew had doubts about the guard's story. But for others it had the ring of truth, especially since the guard had little reason now to tell his tale unless it were true. Most decided this account must have been about Wride, who was a first lieutenant, and who had said that he would rather go down fighting than be taken alive.

Bittersweet Survival

Camp Ōmori was liberated a week later on August 29, 1945. Commander Harold Stassen, with a contingent of Marines, took control of the camp while the event was recorded by newsreel cameramen. Back in America, Garin, who had felt tortured by the feeling that his absence had somehow contributed to the loss of his crew, remembered tearfully the joy he felt when he saw the newsreel of Robert Grant cheering with other emaciated POWs. Some of his comrades had survived after all. Norman Kruvant, however, who had been sent back to the States a few days after being escorted off the runway on July 19, was even more consumed by feelings of guilt mixed with relief for not being with the crew when it went down over Niigata. Upon returning and learning about his brother's death, Kruvant suffered a complete nervous breakdown from which he never recovered. He died a few years later, an unseen casualty of war.[13]

Robert Grant (right, wearing hat) during the liberation of Camp Ōmori.
(Reuters/ITN.)

The Jordan Crew was taken to the hospital ship Benevolence for a checkup and then they were brought back to shore and flown to Okinawa. After resting there for a few days and gorging themselves on ice cream, they took a ship to the Philippines via Tinian. When they came to port in Tinian many on the base came out to see their friends. 'Porky' Jordan was porky no more. One of his closest friends, Lt. Sam Parks, was shocked when he saw how much weight Jordan had lost. Parks noted that Jordan walked with the air of a broken man. When asked what had happened, Jordan looked numbly into the distance and muttered, ghostlike, 'I just couldn't eat that damn rotten fish.'[14]

The crew continued on to the Philippines where they met former POWs who had been liberated from Niigata Camp 5B. There they traded stories about what they had heard from the camp guards about their capture and of the fate of their crewmen who had died. From them the Crew heard stories of how civilians had killed the crewmen by beating and then hanging them.[15] After a period of recuperation and relaxation in Manila, they were debriefed by Army Air Force officers and then Military Intelligence personnel about their last mission, capture and subsequent treatment. Everyone on the crew was then given a promotion and put on a slow ship back to the States. As they arrived each said their last goodbyes. Although a few would run into each other on later military assignments or chat briefly at conventions for the 6th Bomb Group many years later, it was the last time for all the survivors of the Jordan Crew to ever see each other again. From San Francisco they parted ways and were sent to various bases across the United States. Within six months, most had returned to civilian life.

---

[1] Robert Michelson, interview by Thomas Saylor (Apple Valley, Minnesota, November 2, 2001), *Prisoner of War Oral History Project: World War Two and Korea* (2001-2002), http://people.csp.edu/saylor/POWproject/POWinterviews/MichelsonR.htm. (accessed February 7, 2006).

[2] Robert Grant, interview by author, April 23, 2004, MD Recording. Paul Trump, interview by author, September 13, 2004, MD Recording.

[3] Paul Trump, September 13, 2004.

[4] Yuichi Hatto, interview by author, February 22, 2005, Tokyo, MD Recording.

[5] Robert Martindale, *The 13th Mission* (Austin, Texas: Eakin Press, 1998), 92-94.

[6] Paul Trump, September 13, 2004.

[7] Peter Henderson and Claire Hadfield, 'Fifty Years Too Late: Death Camp Monster Finally Says I'm Sorry,' *The Mail* (UK), August 20 1995, 5.

[8] Paul Trump, 'War Memories,' 2003, unpublished manuscript (photocopy), 6, Trump Family Papers, Lititz, PA.

[9] Paul Trump, 'War Memories,' 6. Robert Martindale, 236-237. After the war, Provoo was convicted for treason but later acquitted. He became a Buddhist priest and lived in Hawaii until his death in 2001.

[10] Paul Trump, interview by author, March 23, 2004, MD Recording.

[11] Paul Trump, 'War Memories,' 6.

[12] Robert Burkle, 'Affidavit' (Judge Advocate General (Army), Record Group 153, War Crimes Branch Case Files, Case 33-130, 1944-1949, photocopied).

[13] Milton Garin, e-mail message to author, June 6, 2003.

[14] Sam Parks, interview by author, March 20, 2004, MD Recording.

[15] Walter Dickerson, Champaign County, Illinois, Affidavit to War Crimes Office, Civil Affairs Division, October 16, 1947, Private Papers of Robert Neptune, Fiske Hanley Collection, Ft. Worth, Texas. Harry Steen, interview by Charles Roland, September, 1992, interview HCM 11-92, transcript, Oral History Archives, Hannah Chair for the History of Medicine, McMaster University, Hamilton, Ontario, Canada.

PART THREE

THE COVER-UP

CHAPTER ELEVEN

BURYING THE EVIDENCE

The war was over. After the initial shock had passed, many in Niigata City breathed a collective sigh of relief – their lives had been spared. A feeling of euphoria swept over the city, which was soon followed by celebrations. B-29s began to make food drops over Niigata. Allied POWs and local citizens shared what they had and began to eat and drink together. The POWs who had been in Niigata throughout the war were in a different category than the hated fliers who had mined their seas and cursed their skies. Now that the military dictatorship had collapsed Niigata citizens were free to express their true feelings to the captives in their midst. Tokukichi Kumagaya remembers:

> I guess we had a kind of inferiority complex toward the Westerners. We called them 'hairy ones,' but we felt a kind of admiration turned to prejudice. We didn't want to lose to the whites. Like a lot of people, I didn't hate Americans. That's why the government had to make up slogans to promote hatred. They said the Americans and the British were the Anglo-American Demons. We fought a war against America without any genuine hostility. Maybe the professional soldiers felt a strong rivalry, but not us workers.[1]

A former Allied prisoner from Niigata POW Camp 5B, Doug Idlett, recalled how a few days after the surrender he and a couple of campmates had wandered into downtown Niigata at dusk. While they were walking around and taking in the sights suddenly from around a corner came three Japanese soldiers in full battle gear. They were roaring drunk, but when they saw the American POWs they froze, standing and staring wide-eyed at Idlett and his friends, who were terrified. After what seemed to be several agonizingly long seconds the soldiers suddenly erupted in bawdy laughter and began slapping Idlett and his friends on the back. The soldiers then took them out for drinks. For Idlett the experience was surreal. Only a couple of days earlier these soldiers would have killed them. Now, simply on the word of the Emperor, they had become friends.[2]

These early days helped, for a time at least, to cover up the feelings of confusion that simmered under the surface for Niigata's residents. The world had been turned upside down with the Emperor's radio broadcast. Who was in charge now? No one knew what would happen, but the fear was that Niigata would soon be flooded with American Occupation Forces. Stories spread that when they came the Americans would be an avenging army. The men of Niigata would be castrated and used like farm animals while their wives and daughters would become comfort women for the conquerors.[3] Such acts had been committed by their own military during the war and it was natural to assume that now it would be their turn. These rumors were especially worrying to the villagers in Yakeyama.

The Committal

Ten days after the crash, Keiichi Meguro, the village ward, had called a meeting.[4] He had heard the stories of how at least two of the fliers had fought back with their weapons – with fatal consequences. He was there at the Kyōgase Village Hall and at the crash site when the cut and battered body of one crewman had been taken back to Yakeyama.[5] The question now was how to dispose of the bodies. The villagers debated the issue for some time. Some suggested burning the bodies since they were the remains of, as propaganda broadcasts had often stated, demonic beasts (*kichiku-bei-ei*). This idea was rejected, since symbolically it was too similar to their Buddhist funeral rites. Most urged for the bodies to be thrown into the nearby Agano River. However, Sgt. Chūzo Sato, a wounded war veteran who had recently returned from the fronts in China and who was at home awaiting reassignment, vehemently opposed this plan. Sato's right hand had been injured, something that was commonly the result of someone who had had enough of the killing and who had wanted to return home. He spoke at length, exhorting the villagers to treat the bodies of the American fliers with a modicum of respect since they had died with honor and had been brave enough to fly so deeply into enemy territory. Also, because every Japanese citizen was a soldier (*kokumin kaihei*), he warned the villagers not to do anything that would violate the spirit of Bushido.[6]

It was eventually decided that the bodies would be buried. The bodies were dragged out close to the village crematorium. While graves were being dug some villagers again started to beat the bodies. Spero's head was crushed. The bodies of Spero and Adams were placed vertically in each grave. After they were buried, the mostly cremated remains of Wride and Hawkins were each dumped on top of Adams and Spero's graves. As a final gesture of loathing several used the open graves as a public toilet before the remains were finally completely buried.[7]

Growing Concern in the Villages

At the beginning of September 1945, one month after this grisly burial had taken place, the American Occupation Forces arrived in Niigata City. Patrols began to be seen in the countryside. It was only a matter of time before someone would hear rumors and come to Yokogōshi to find out about the B-29 and its crew. In fact, they had already been told.

Teitaro Sato, who had been at the Kyōgase Town Hall and participated in the capture of the twenty-two year old member of the Jordan Crew, began to lose sleep about his fate under the new Occupation.

A rumor spread around the town, 'Sato will be imprisoned in Okinawa as a war criminal for torturing the American soldier.' On the street, people looked at me and murmured, 'He's still here.' After a while, I began to worry, and after much struggling, finally decided to go to the military government in Niigata and talk to them in person. On September 7, I rode a bicycle from Suibara to Niigata. When I arrived at the command center of the occupation army, two MPs were standing at the gate with their guns. I told them about the purpose of my visit, but we couldn't communicate. After a little while, an interpreter came out. I told him what had really happened. I said, 'I rescued an American soldier who had bailed out, and followed my order by escorting him to the emergency headquarters, pushing out an excited, violent throng of people.' I also asked him if the rumor of me being sent to and imprisoned on Okinawa was true. The interpreter went back inside, and brought someone who looked like an officer. After they talked, the interpreter told me to go home in the tone of an order, and shut the door as if to get rid of me. I remember how badly my bottom hurt for days after riding on a bicycle round-trip from Suibara to Niigata.[8]

Because the brutal *kempei-tai* had been their only working model for how a military investigation would be conducted, the villagers were terrified by the prospect of what the Americans might do once word got out about the fate of the crewmen. Now that Sato had gone to throw himself on the mercy of the Americans, time was running out.

A Cunning Plan

Meguro called another meeting. After another lengthy debate Meguro proposed a strategy that was being used successfully in other parts of Japan. The bodies were to be exhumed and moved to his vegetable patch on the edge of the village. Men would cut posts and fashion them into monuments and bring soil from their gardens to make mounds over the graves. Women would gather bamboo, not to make spears, but now to make a fence to enclose the graves. Children would gather chrysanthemums and decorate the graves. The villagers threw themselves into the work and very soon a respectable gravesite had been set up. When the time came, Meguro would be the front man who would protect the village from any harm.[9]

The Approach of the Americans

Teitaro Sato's visit to the Occupation Headquarters in Niigata had been ignored. On a cold and rainy Sunday afternoon near the end of September a patrol of the

27th Infantry Division was making its way down the banks of the Agano River near Yakeyama Village. Valery Burati, who was with the patrol, remembers the event.

> Keichi Meguro, the village master, met us quite by accident on the dike above his house. Through our interpreter he learned our purpose. He hurriedly excused himself, ran down the lee side of the dike to his house and came panting back with a bouquet of yellow flowers.
>
> The jeeps whined in the mud until we left them and walked down a narrow path the farmers used to their vegetable gardens. It was not far, when we came in view of a small wooden shelter filled with straw on a rise of ground. Meguro ran ahead. Bamboo and cryptomeria trees rose behind the shack. In front of it a pretty Japanese farm girl huddled over a straw fire which sent up a smudge but little heat. Behind the shelter, and between it and the cryptomeria grove, we saw two plain wooden pillars, neatly made, enclosed by a bamboo railing. Meguro, sloshing in pools of water, was ostentatiously arranging his bouquets among others already in front of the wooden markers.
>
> 'We moved them here from the place they fell because this part of the land is above the floods,' he said. 'The two who could be identified are under the post at the right; the two who were burned are at the left.' Our interpreter translated the markers, 'Grave of the American Soldiers, July 20, 1945, Yokogōshi Village.'
>
> I studied the wooden markers and the bamboo fence. Both were weather beaten and stained. Certainly they had been placed there before September when our first troops arrived.[10]

Burati writes feeling overwrought with thoughts of the stark loneliness of this gravesite and of how these men had died so far from home. He tried to cover his emotions, and through the translator, spoke in a friendly manner with Meguro before returning to Niigata to report the incident. Burati's feelings, however, did not go unnoticed by Meguro. Word spread quickly that the first encounter with the American soldiers had gone well. Teitaro Sato explains.

> The Ward Director [Meguro] had his wits about him. He had laid flowers on the mounds of dirt at the edge of the village. The American soldiers were so moved by the site, they concluded that no war crimes or acts of brutality had been committed...Hearing this, I felt greatly relieved, and was deeply grateful to the Ward Director for his wits and compassion.[11]

It would be another month before more soldiers would return, this time, armed with questions.

---

[1] Haruko Taya Cook and Theodore F. Cook, *Japan at War: An Oral History* (New York: The New Press, 2000), 50.

[2] Doug Idlett, interview by author, March 25, 2004, MD Recording.

[3] 佐藤貞太郎 (Teitaro Sato), 'B-29 撃墜余談 (Digressions about the B-29 Downing),' 五頭郷土文化 (*Gozu Hometown Culture*) 7 (December, 1984), 62.

[4] Yoshio Ito, interview by Toshihide Uemura, July 1, 1998, tape recording, The B-29 Downing Incident (B29 撃墜事件について), Former Yokogōshi City History Department, Yokogōshi, Niigata.

[5] Chuzo Sato, interview by Toshihide Uemura, July 1, 1998, tape recording, The B-29 Downing Incident (B29 撃墜事件について), Former Yokogōshi City History Department, Yokogōshi, Niigata.

[6] Anonymous B, e-mail message to author, August 6, 2003.

[7] Anonymous B, August 6, 2003.

[8] 佐藤貞太郎 (Teitaro Sato), 62-63.

[9] Anonymous B, interview by author, June 20, 2003, notes. Yoshio Ito, July 1, 1998.

[10] Valery Burati, 'Fragments of a Mission,' 1972, unpublished manuscript (typewritten), 4-5, George McGraw Private Papers, Gillett, Arkansas.

[11] 佐藤貞太郎 (Teitaro Sato), 63.

CHAPTER TWELVE

THE INVESTIGATION BEGINS

In early December an investigative team from Tokyo arrived in Yokogōshi. Their jeeps had even more difficulty than Burati's patrol a month earlier, as now the narrow roads, difficult to negotiate during the best of times, were covered with the deep wet snow that is characteristic of Niigata's 'Snow Country'.[1]

One of the team members was a young Lieutenant by the name of Robert T. Groh. Groh, from New York City, had served most of the war as one of Franklin D. Roosevelt's secret service bodyguards. When Roosevelt died all of his bodyguards were drafted. Groh began as an attorney on the staff of General MacArthur and was with the first regiment of American troops to occupy Tokyo. Two months later he was assigned to Niigata to make preliminary reports and to search for Japanese soldiers who had mistreated American POWs. During the year he was based in Niigata, Groh was zealous in his efforts to arrest former POW camp personnel and bring them to justice, as evidenced by his first visit to the deserted Allied POW Camps of Niigata 5B and 15B.

Picture from the gate of Niigata POW Camp 5B taken during Lt. Robert Groh's investigation. Dickerson was held briefly at this camp before joining the rest of the Jordan Crew on the train to Tokyo.
(NARA.)

Upon arriving in Niigata with my contingent of men we dispersed and examined the actual bunks where the men were kept. There were writings on the wall, none of which were discernable. In one of the cells there was a drawing of a man, Japanese and bald, who the American prisoners nicknamed 'Egghead'. I then assembled the Niigata police and told the Chief of Police that I would give him 72 hours to produce 'Egghead' to me or else I would arrest him [the chief] and take him in, but I wasn't going back to headquarters empty handed. Sure enough I received notification from the police that they had 'Egghead' and they handed him over to me at the train station. I arrested him and went back to Tokyo to see that he was brought to trial.[2]

Some time later the team went to Yakeyama where they inspected the gravesite, took pictures and interviewed Meguro about the fate of the crewmen. Meguro told them that the plane had crashed in the nearby sweet potato field. When he could get close enough to the crash site he found four bodies in the rear of the plane. He and others from the village removed these bodies from the plane and buried them on his land. He added that he had been the custodian of the graves ever since.[3] Because it was the dead of winter it would be impossible for Mortuary Services to recover the remains and send them to the States until next spring. In the interim Groh and the team would return to Niigata to verify Meguro's story. At the time Groh had little reason to disbelieve the story that all had died in the crash and saw the actions of the villagers as very considerate.[4]

Robert Groh inspecting the graves containing
the remains of Adams, Spero, Hawkins and Wride.
(Investigative Division Reports #226.)

Incident at the Elementary School

Given its conspicuous absence from the fields near Yakeyama, the next step was to discover the fate of Jordan's B-29. Groh and others scoured the countryside. When it was discovered that .50 caliber machine guns from the rear of the B-29 were being displayed as a war trophy over at the Yokogōshi Elementary school, the team went to collect them. After arriving, however, an altercation arose between the investigation team and the school's Principal.

Principals during this era wielded an enormous amount of unchallenged authority in their schools. This one obviously did not appreciate Americans coming into his school uninvited and throwing their weight around. The team stated that the machine guns were American military property; it would not do to allow these weapons to remain in the hands of a recently-defeated enemy. The guns were to be turned over – immediately.

There are several versions about what happened next. One version of the tale is that the Principal refused to turn the guns over, having locked them in a room where they kept equipment for students' science experiments. Another version is that the Principal didn't understand what the soldiers wanted at first and later couldn't find the key to the storage room. Regardless of what really happened, the team left, contacted the city authorities, and within a very short time the Principal was fired.[5] The guns were then collected and taken to Niigata Iron Works where they were melted down. 'This is the sorrow of a defeated country,' said the Principal as he left the school.[6] Villagers still remember him as symbolic of their own shattered identity during those days.

Word spread about the fate of their local Principal, causing some villagers to run out of their huts and throw what pieces they had collected from the B-29 into the nearby Agano River. A few days later, Meguro showed up at the Niigata Occupation Headquarters with the plane's four propellers.[7]

A few hidden pieces of Jordan's B-29 still remain in Yakeyama. Even now, every few years or so, a declining number of the senior citizens will bring what bits they have left from their secret places, and with many sad sighs, show them to the young ones.[8]

Following a Faint Paper Trail

Over the next few months, in between his numerous trips to Tokyo and inspections of POW campsites in rural Niigata, Groh interviewed former soldiers of the *kempei-tai*, police officers, staff at the *Niigata Nippo* newspaper, and villagers in Yokogōshi about the downing of Jordan's B-29. All provided essentially the same story that the crewmen had died in the crash and none of the captured members of the Jordan Crew had been mistreated. Groh also retrieved the Missing Air Crew Report on the Jordan Crew, though this early version of the report did not contain the surviving crew's casualty questionnaire forms that they had filled out in the Philippines. He found newspaper stories from the *Niigata Nippo*, local police reports, and one letter from a Yonero Shimada in Tokyo. Although Groh does not mention Shimada's status, it is likely that, from the information in his letter, Shimada had been a soldier stationed in Niigata and possibly a guard at one of the Niigata POW Camps. In his note, Shimada stated that three crewmen who had parachuted from the B-29 on the evening of July 20 had been murdered and robbed by soldiers from the 9th Platoon of the 1993rd Regiment.[9] These soldiers, the letter explained, were on anti-aircraft duty near Niitsu City, not far from Yokogōshi. Shimada also provided a list of soldiers' names who he claimed had participated in the killings.

Groh was not inclined to believe this letter. It seemed obvious to him that the crew had perished in the crash. 'The only possibility of foul play,' wrote Groh, 'lies in the fact that three of the four in the graves were murdered prior to burial. Although this is highly improbable, it can only be proved conclusively by re-opening the graves and examining the bodies for evidence of foul play.'[10]

Opening the Graves

By late April 1946 the winter snows had receded and the ground had softened. Together with a team of four soldiers, former Japanese soldiers and 2nd Lt. John Reitze from the Memorial Branch of the Quartermaster General, Groh went to exhume the bodies. As they went down the bumpy roads to Yakeyama, Groh began feeling apprehensive. He was not looking forward to viewing the contents of the graves.[11]

Reitze was in charge of the recovery unit. As required by the Quartermaster General he had conducted a separate investigation into the crash and the fate of the crewmen. Reitze also interviewed Meguro, who again stated that all four had died in the crash. However, Meguro changed his story; this time he said that there had been two bodies in the front of the plane who were partially cremated and two in the back who had been only slightly burned.[12]

The soldiers split into two groups and began to dig. Nervous villagers watched from a distance. About five feet down, they began to find body parts. To ease their discomfort the soldiers made a game of the task by calling out the parts they found. 'I found part of an arm!' 'I got a femur.'[13]

The bodies of Adams and Spero were more intact, which surprised the villagers as they saw their bodies being lifted from the graves. Some speculated that because Americans are bread eaters their bodies do not decompose as quickly as the Japanese.[14] Nevertheless, because they had been buried for over seven months in the sandy, watery, acidic soil of the village, they were, in the eyes of Groh and the recovery team, in an advanced state of decomposition. The only way they could be identified was from identity tags in their clothing.

A Tense Moment

Groh had instructed the team to be careful to examine the bodies for any signs that any of the crewmen had been murdered. Spero's skull had been crushed – the team assumed this had happened in the plane crash. Adam's body had a broken leg. Meguro was called up to explain this. He told them that this body had been hanging on a machine gun spindle inside the plane.[15] The team also noticed rope marks on Spero and Adams and asked if they had been tortured. Meguro and others in the village explained that the bodies had been put on stretchers and their arms were tied with rope so that they wouldn't hang down.[16] This was accepted by the team and Reitz reported later that there had been no concrete evidence discovered that would point to anything else but death from the crash.[17]

The remains were photographed, tagged, and placed in new wooden caskets. The villagers were filled with wonder by the gentleness with which the soldiers treated the remains, and envious of the work gloves that the soldiers threw away after having used them only once.[18] Darker feelings of jealousy rumbled deeper. Caught between the *kempei-tai* of the past and the Occupation Forces of the present, looked down upon by the city folk and generally ignored except for the times when they were bullied by the powers that be, no one had treated them with the same consideration and tenderness that these rotten corpses were now receiving.[19] But such feelings were hidden behind smiles as the soldiers loaded the bodies into the truck.

Wary Peace Offerings

After the team had finished putting away the bodies, they turned and offered something to the villagers called chocolate. The villagers were afraid to touch it. It was black and might be some sort of poison to punish them. The soldiers ate some of the chocolate to show them it was safe. They cautiously accepted the chocolate but didn't eat it until much later. When they did, they were shocked by its intense sweetness.[20]

Meguro and others in the village in turn brought out food. Because of the failed rice harvest of 1945 this was a major sacrifice on the part of the villagers. Occupation troops were under orders not to receive food from civilians, so they declined at first. The villagers thought the soldiers were also afraid of poison, and ate some of the food to show that it was safe. With this ritual of mutual goodwill thus fulfilled, both sides felt a measure of ease with each other and sat down to eat. Based upon interviews with residents in Yakeyama, historian Tomoyuki Kanazuka narrates the event:

> The soldiers started to enjoy themselves; some uttered a few Japanese words they knew such as *arigato*, *tōfu*, and *sake*, while others were trying hard to eat tofu with chopsticks, and touching and appreciating the *kutani-yaki* sake cups. There was rather a friendly atmosphere there. The soldiers left, thanking the villagers for their kindness, repeating 'thank you' and '*arigato*', bowing in the Japanese way.[21]

Groh also remembers the merry picnic held near the graves. But he had had little inclination to participate. The gruesome sight of the exhumed bodies left him feeling nauseous, and he was unable to eat anything for the rest of the day.[22]

138

[1] Masao Saito, interview by Toshihide Uemura, July 1, 1998, tape recording, The B-29 Downing Incident (B29 撃墜事件について), Former Yokogōshi City History Department, Yokogōshi, Niigata.

[2] Robert T. Groh, Quogue, New York, letter to author, August 18, 2004.

[3] 'Investigation Division Reports #226' (GHQ/SCAP Records. Record Group 331: National Archives and Records Service, March 1946 - April 1948. NARA, Washington DC, photocopied).

[4] Robert T. Groh, September 17, 2004.

[5] Yoshikazu Nakamura, interview by Toshihide Uemura, July 1, 1998, tape recording, The B-29 Downing Incident (B29 撃墜事件について), Former Yokogōshi City History Department, Yokogōshi, Niigata.

[6] Masao Saito, July 1, 1998. Yoshikazu Nakamura, July 1, 1998.

[7] 'Investigation Division Reports #226.'

[8] 'American soldiers surrounded by spear-wielding villagers (竹やりの村民米兵囲む),' Niigata Nippo, August 12, 2000.

[9] 'Investigation Division Reports #226.'

[10] 'Investigation Division Reports #226.'

[11] Robert T. Groh, September 17, 2004. Masao Saito, July 1, 1998.

[12] John Reitze (2nd Lt.), 'Report of Recovery Team 1 (T1J27-141)' (HQ Eighth Army APO 343, Memorial Branch, Quartermaster General, 1946, photocopied).

[13] Robert T. Groh, September 17, 2004.

[14] Masao Saito, July 1, 1998.

[15] John Reitze (2nd Lt.).

[16] Masao Saito, July 1, 1998.

[17] John Reitze (2nd Lt.).

[18] 金塚友之丞 (Tomoyuki Kanazuka), '横越村焼山へ落ちた B29 と京ヶ瀬村へ降りた落下傘 (The B-29 that went down in Yokogōshi and those who parachuted into Kyōgase),' 郷土新潟 (Hometown Niigata) 6 (February, 1965), 11.

[19] Motoichi Fujita, Tadashi Saito, Hikaru Sato, interview by author, January 16, 2004, MD Recording.

[20] Motoichi Fujita, Tadashi Saito, Hikaru Sato, January 16, 2004.

[21] 金塚友之丞 (Tomoyuki Kanazuka), 12.

[22] Robert T. Groh, August 18, 2004.

CHAPTER THIRTEEN

THE INVESTIGATION'S LAST DAYS

The remains of the four dead Jordan Crew members were sent to Yokohama where an autopsy was performed to confirm the identity of the bodies. There was no investigation into whether the wounds they had suffered had taken place before or after they died. The assumption was that the crew had died in the crash. Even if there had been suspicions, with literally hundreds of remains coming in from various parts of Japan, there was little time to perform anything but the most basic of autopsies.

The identity of the bodies of Adams and Spero was verified and the remains were soon sent to their families. It was virtually impossible positively to identify the remains of Wride and Hawkins since they were partially cremated. It was only by a process of elimination that the Army's Identification Section concluded that the remains were indeed theirs. These were buried in the military cemetery in Yokohama for a time until shipped to their respective families in the United States.[1]

The case would have been closed at this point had it not been for the discovery of affidavits from survivors of the Jordan Crew. These were taken by other war crimes investigators who were making a case against the staff of the *kempei-tai* headquarters in Tokyo, but some of the crew's accounts mentioned the circumstances surrounding their capture in Niigata as well. Of special interest was Burkle's account from the camp guard in Ōmori. Several letters from Japanese residents also came in, including one that was written by a lady named Kimiko Imai. In it she discussed details of the crew's capture and of their mistreatment by spear-wielding villagers.[2] Since Groh was often on assignment to various sites as part of his other investigations, different investigators were given the Jordan Crew's case. Based on this and other unavailable documents that are only hinted at in the archives, one of the investigators, Capt. William Gill, concluded, 'in view of the fact that several letters have been written by Japanese in the Niigata area, it is believed that at least one murder did take place.'[3]

Pressure on the Village Ward

Meguro was brought to the Niigata office and interrogated several times. While many of the reports in the US Archives contain transcripts of interviews and interrogations that were conducted during such investigations, these materials are missing from files concerning the investigation of the Jordan Crew incident. A summary of these interrogations states that Meguro had changed his story about the location of the bodies in the airplane, but the investigative reports do not seem to highlight this as significant. Years later, Meguro's widow recalls those days as, '…a nightmare. They [the investigators] kept asking over and over if he [Meguro] had murdered the crewmen. I only hoped they would understand.'[4] In another interview, Meguro's widow admits that she (and by implication, her husband) had heard the stories from other villagers about how three had been murdered. Her recollection from visiting the crash site early at dawn was that there were two crewmen lying outside the plane, wearing their caps, and with their side arms in their hands.[5] The accounts of others who were informally interviewed also differed from the version of events given by Meguro to the investigators. For example, in Val Burati's account, Shunkichi Shimizu stated that the two bodies (those of Adams and Spero) had been 'thrown clear' of the plane.[6] Others said they were laying side-by-side inside the plane. Meguro had told other investigators that one body had been hanging on a machine gun spindle. The investigators seemed to have suspected that something was afoot, but without hard evidence or a witness who would come forward, there was little they could do but let Meguro go. Next on the list was Kimiko Imai.

An Unstable Witness

Kimiko Imai was the daughter of a bicycle shop owner in Suibara Village. The people in her community thought of her as one of their local lunatics. Her appearance was peculiar because she was taller than most ladies her age and her hair was a slightly lighter shade than what was considered acceptable. Imai was the same lady who had been arrested by the *kempei-tai* on the morning after the crash.[7] This was a key point that investigators were unaware of during their investigation.

The summary of the investigation states that Imai was also interviewed on several occasions. It seems that in the beginning she had potential for being a witness upon which to build a case. But in subsequent interrogations she exhibited behavior that struck the investigators in Niigata as 'insane' and 'demented.'[8] In later interrogations Imai began to disavow any direct knowledge of the events, stating they were only stories that she had heard from others in the community.

Cold Case File

Imai was at best an unreliable witness. Discussions with Japan Rail officials confirmed that seven of the eleven crewmen boarded the train to Tokyo on July 20. Four had died. Without the bodies available for a full autopsy and no hard evidence, investigators at the Niigata Office were forced to return to Groh's assertion that Adams, Spero, Hawkins and Wride had probably perished in the crash after all. The affidavits they had collected from the surviving members of the Jordan Crew were hearsay, since none had actually seen any of their comrades killed. Grant was the last to see Adams and Spero, and both were still in the plane when he bailed out. In the front of the cabin, Trump was the last to see Hawkins and Wride as he bailed out through the flaming bomb bay. The interrogations, as their final report stated, uncovered many inconsistencies, but the accumulated statements were not solid enough to refute the strong probability of crash-related death.[9]

The case was closed in late 1948. At about this time Shunkichi Shimizu gave Val Burati the pictures that he had taken. Burati had kept these for many years until he tracked down George McGraw in 1970 to give him copies and find out if he knew any other details about the incident. It is unknown whether investigators had seen these pictures. If they did, then the photos are in a classified section of the national archives. The original negatives were lost when the *Niigata Nippo* office was destroyed in the Great Fire of Niigata of 1955.

In the final analysis, the conclusion of the investigators was the only one they could have reached, based upon the evidence they may have had at the time. While their memos indicate a strong suspicion of foul play, they operated under American legal jurisprudence, that suspects are innocent until proven guilty. Solid proof was the one thing that was in short supply, and with the exception of the letter written by Yonero Shimada in Tokyo, the investigators did not have names or any idea about who might have killed the lost airmen of the Jordan Crew. On that early morning of July 20, in darkened rice paddies, there were numerous bands of villagers, many of them women, who were throwing rocks and thrusting wildly with their spears. It is possible that nobody knew who struck the fatal blow. An additional barrier to solving the case was that Yakeyama and the surrounding hamlets were small, tight-knit farming communities. Many of the residents were related to each other by blood if not by marriage. What hope did investigators have of inducing someone to come forward to tell what they knew? Even if they could find the perpetrators, did the Occupation Forces really want to be seen as harassing old ladies and housewives? There were other high-profile cases that were still open and needing to be prosecuted. It was best to move on.

And so, the smoking embers of the investigation were finally allowed to grow cold. The dead were buried. Silence fell over the villages and the farmers returned to their fields.

---

[1] 'Individual Deceased Personnel File: Florio D. Spero (USAAF 36785915), Adams, Max A. (USAAF 14098594), Wride, Clinton L. (USAAF 0666112), Hawkins, Wails (USAAF 0825628)' (Alexandria, VA: Casualty and Memorial Affairs Operations Center, Mortuary Affairs and Casualty Support Division, photocopied).

[2] 'Investigative Division Reports #472' (GHQ/SCAP Records. Record Group 331, National Archives and Records Service, May 1946 - March 1947. NARA, Washington DC, photocopied).

[3] 'Investigative Division Reports #472.'

[4] 'American soldiers surrounded by spear-wielding villagers (竹やりの村民米兵囲む),' *Niigata Nippo*, August 12, 2000.

[5] Miyo Meguro, interview by Toshihide Uemura, July 1, 1998, tape recording, The B-29 Downing Incident (B29 撃墜事件について), Former Yokogōshi City History Department, Yokogōshi, Niigata.

[6] Valery Burati, 'Fragments of a Mission,' 1972, unpublished manuscript (typewritten), 3, George McGraw Private Papers, Gillett, Arkansas.

[7] Yoshikazu Nakamura, interview by Toshihide Uemura, July 1, 1998, tape recording, The B-29 Downing Incident (B29 撃墜事件について), Former Yokogōshi City History Department, Yokogōshi, Niigata.

[8] 'Investigation Division Reports #226' (GHQ/SCAP Records. Record Group 331: National Archives and Records Service, March 1946 - April 1948. NARA, Washington DC, photocopied).

[9] 'Investigation Division Reports #226.'

CHAPTER FOURTEEN

RECONSTRUCTING THE LAST MOMENTS

A number of questions arise when reading the accounts of the Jordan Crew during the last days of the war, the stories of eyewitnesses immediately following the war, and the memories of those who spoke out in the twilight years of their lives. What reason would the *kempei-tai* officers have had to lie to the captive Jordan Crew about the fate of their lost comrades? Given the inconsistencies in the accounts of Meguro and others, why didn't the investigators in Niigata work harder to find out what had happened? Why didn't the investigators follow up on the lead provided in the letter by Yonero Shimada? Most of the people who might know the answers to these questions are no longer with us.

Inconsistent Testimony

Except for the cursory mention in one police report that a couple of the crewmen were 'injured', the Japanese reports found in Niigata by investigators portray the Jordan Crew's capture in terms of procedures, timetables, professionalism, and of the Crew's steady movement away from the crash site towards Tokyo.[1] This last point is significant as it hints of older rumblings between Niigata and the Imperial Government, the implication being that the Tokyo leadership, not the citizens of Niigata, should be held accountable for anything that may have happened on July 20. It is safe to assume that the 'fear factor' of what might happen under the new Occupation kept many from giving full and truthful testimony. For that reason, I have chosen to focus on the stories told before the war's end and those that were given many years later. In these instances, there was little fear of reprisals, and I believe these versions have a higher probability of being more truthful, though not necessarily more consistent.

Once the element of fear is removed, the story becomes one of crewmen killed in the heat of the moment. The themes that emerge from these accounts feature images such as fire, fear, anger, gunfire, spears, beatings, ropes, hooks, blood, screams, and death. With the time it took for soldiers to reach the Kyōgase Town Hall, the wartime agitation of the local villagers, and the fact that many B-29 crewmen were killed elsewhere in Japan after bailing out, it is reasonable to assume that some of Jordan's Crew could have been killed by villagers, especially when one takes into consideration that at least three who were killed had vowed that they would either not be taken alive or never bail out over Japan.

Eyewitnesses have placed Keiichi Meguro at various locations where it is certain that he was privy to far more information than what he gave to the American investigators. His accounts of what happened at the crash site were contradictory and at times factually incorrect. Meguro's account to Lt. Reitze about finding one of the bodies hanging on a machine gun spindle was physically impossible. According to Robert Grant the spindle is located within an inaccessible part of the weapon.[2] Based upon the accounts of the *kempei-tai* to the Jordan Crew immediately after their capture and those of elderly villagers collected for this book it is probable that two, possibly three, crewmen were not in the plane when it crashed. However, as the various accounts of the dead crewmen were repeated they became increasingly linked to deaths caused by the crash. Today, the account given by Meguro has become the foundation for local folklore, even when contradictions crop up among various storytellers.

I had my own experience with this clash between oral tradition and history during my interview in Yakeyama. The elderly men spoke in great detail about the crash and, as their stories shifted to the fate of the dead crewmen, all spoke about how one had died when he had bailed out and his parachute had not opened in time. Later, however, they spoke of approaching the plane in the morning and of finding two bodies in the rear cabin. They were laying side-by-side in the cabin and both of their parachutes were half-opened. It was obvious, they said, that the crewmen had died in the crash.

In most of my interviews, I tended to let people speak as much as possible, but before I could catch myself I blurted out the obvious. 'If at least one of the crewmen had died after bailing out, how did he get back into the plane?'

The men were stunned by the question. They had mostly been talking and reminiscing among themselves with me as a quiet spectator, but now all turned their eyes to me with stares cold and hostile. It was a moment of considerable discomfort. A local Japanese historian who had set up the meeting and who had accompanied me during the interviews, recognized my peril and quickly inserted, 'Oh, but he was brought back to the plane from somewhere else, right?' The men looked visibly relieved: 'Oh, yes, that's right. That's right. That's how it was. He was dead when we found him, though.' Everyone's face was saved, the local legend was preserved, and I ventured no more questions.[3]

Murky Clues

Although the earliest news is not always the most accurate, the only constant found in all of the historical accounts studied was that one member of the crew had gone down with the plane. This body was found in the smoking ruins in the early hours after the fires had burned themselves out. With the exception of these remains, however, all of the other bodies were highly mobile and described by eyewitnesses in different places at different times.

It was only later that the second body of the crewman was 'found' next to the charred remains of the man in the copilot's seat, and these accounts came after various bands of air raid wardens and other groups of villagers had been seen going back and forth from the wreckage. The earliest accounts of those who were at the crash site just before sunrise call into question later reports of this body being cremated in the crash. It was described as having blue eyes and leaning against the wreckage. Others remember him still wearing his cap, clutching a pistol and in possession of navigation maps. These remains were likely those of Wride. A study of his medical files shows that Wride had blue eyes (but so did Adams), and as a bombardier he would have had navigation maps.

In the picture obtained by Val Burati showing the disposition of the bodies of Spero and Adams a careful examination reveals that Spero is tied to a sled with his arms bound behind his back as if he had been captured. The legs are blackened, which could have resulted from being burned and the head, while wounded, is not crushed.

Most certainly, it is difficult to tell much from this grainy picture about the possible causes of death of these two crewmen, and it is equally possible Spero and Adams' wounds could have resulted from the crash. The photo was shown to a family member of the author who had been an undertaker for over forty years and who had viewed hundreds of people who had perished from many different circumstances, including from plane crashes. He was told nothing of this research and was asked for his opinion regarding what kind of deaths they appeared to be. His opinion was that Adam's wounds look very similar to the type of blunt force trauma that a body suffers in auto accidents or some other type of crash.[4] If this theory is correct, then it might have been the case that Adams had taken too long in putting on his parachute and by the time he bailed out there was not enough time for his parachute to open safely. This would also help explain why his leg was broken. However, and mysteriously, in the account of Teitaro Sato of the crewman that he had helped capture, he noted that this crewman acknowledged that he was twenty-two years old. After an exhaustive search through the archives and military records, I discovered that, on the date of the Jordan Crew's capture, Max Adams was the only one on the crew who was twenty-two years of age.

If the account by Sato is factual, then the attack of the villagers and the massive head wounds which he described might account for wounds seen on Adams. Sato reveals that the villagers in Kyōgase had some knowledge about the torture of crewmen in the town hall. Torture to Japanese at the time would entail something far more brutal than slapping or beatings. Slapping and striking the head was so common as to be standard treatment during those days. Some form of torture could account for Adam's broken leg.

Only an autopsy could have determined when Adam's wounds had occurred, but by the time the investigators began to look into the possibility of whether some of the crew had been killed after bailing out, Adams' remains, and the remains of the rest of the crew, had been sent by ship back to the United States.

It would be interesting, therefore, to find out how the investigators in Niigata would have proceeded if they had had access to all of the additional photos and interviews that were gathered during the writing of this book. Given the confusion of the early morning of July 20, it is likely they would have concluded that nothing certain could be deduced from the data which I have collected. Nevertheless, based upon my three years of painstaking research on this incident, I will venture to offer the following reconstruction of what may have happened.

Returning to that Night

Trump had just bailed out through the flames that were licking the interior of the cabin. After trying to reason with Hawkins, Wride then bailed out of the plane. Hawkins kept the B-29 aloft for as long as possible to give any other crewmen who might still be on board a chance to get out before the inevitable. When the wing snapped, as a natural reflex, he pulled back on the elevator controls, which did nothing to stop the plane from spinning wildly. It would not be long now. Better this than what awaited those who had just bailed out. Death, however, when it finally came after the downward spiral, may not have been instantaneous. The plane fell only a few hundred meters to the ground, and the tightness of his grip on the controls when his body was wrested from the cockpit later on suggests that he may have suffered considerably before the horrible end.

Because Wride was the last to bail out from the front cabin, Trump could not see him floating above his parachute. However, a group of air raid wardens spotted both parachutes and made their way with haste to the spot where it appeared they would land.

Trump's freefall before he could regain control of his parachute was seen by air wardens, and he fell a further nine meters to sink into the rice paddy. He had hidden himself and his parachute before the air raid wardens finally reached the scene. The air wardens assumed that one crewman had not made it to the ground alive. They would find the body later. Wride, however, landed nearby not long afterwards. He was seen and quickly surrounded. Terrified, he drew his weapon and began shooting wildly before trying to run away. Infuriated, the air raid wardens descended upon him, beating and hacking him to death as he screamed in pain. His body was then searched for anything of value.

The air raid wardens were now in a quandary. Their orders had been to capture, not to kill any survivors. The local police and the *kempei-tai* were feared, and it was uncertain whether they would reward or punish the air raid wardens for what had happened. To hide the evidence, his body was carried back to the burning wreckage and thrown as close as possible to the fire. Wride's body was burned, but not completely.

Spero and Adams bailed out after Grant who, like Trump, would have been unable to see them from under his parachute. Grant landed, and because he was more concerned with dealing with his inflatable life raft, parachute, weapon and finding a place to hide, he did not see Spero landing in the vicinity. A patrol soon came upon Spero, and true to his word, he fought back. After his weapon was empty, Spero was also caught and beaten to death.[5] His body was also dragged back to the plane, where attempts were made to burn his body. These efforts were less successful: His legs were burned, but most of his body and facial features were left intact.

If Adams did not perish from his parachute not opening in time, then he would be the crewman who had been captured by Teitaro Sato's group of air raid wardens. Adams would have been wounded far more seriously than Sato's account described, and after further abuse in the Kyōgase Town Hall, he died or was near death. His body could have been the one which was thrown into the back of the truck and covered. It can be seen in the second photograph of the Jordan Crew in the truck that there is a white sheet in the back, and none of the soldiers are standing in this area. Adams would have been placed here. The truck stopped by the crash site to dump the body before making its way to Kameda and later to Niigata City. The white canvas sheet upon which he was carried would have seemed to some to have been a parachute.

While this reconstruction is highly-speculative, and numerous other variations are also possible, unless additional data or eyewitness accounts are discovered I believe what has been presented is as close as we will ever get to what happened on the outskirts of Niigata early on that morning of July 20, 1945.

---

[1] 'Investigation Division Reports #226' (GHQ/SCAP Records. Record Group 331: National Archives and Records Service, March 1946 - April 1948. NARA, Washington DC, photocopied).

[2] Robert Grant, interview by author, April 23, 2004, MD Recording.

[3] Motoichi Fujita, Tadashi Saito, Hikaru Sato, interview by author, January 16, 2004, MD Recording.

[4] Ronald Hadley, interview by author, November 28, 2005, notes.

[5] Grant first reported in 1945 that the screams he heard came from Spero. Although he retracted this story later, by his own admission, there were many events that occurred on that evening which he maintains that he will not speak of, and promises to carry knowledge of those events to his grave.

EPILOGUE

CHAPTER FIFTEEN

SIXTY YEARS LATER

The Author and Choei Shimizu, son of one of the eyewitnesses to the B-29 crash and owner of the field that contains the crash site.

I am up to my hips in the muddy field where Gordon Jordan's plane went down, participating on the last day of an excavation of the crash site. Together with a local historian from the Yokogōshi Municipal Department of History and the son of one of the farmers who witnessed the crash over half a century ago, we dig through the rich topsoil to find a layer of blue powder that has a decidedly poisonous look. The fields had been unusable for over twenty years from these chemicals that bled from the burning plane. For many seasons, even weeds would not grow there.[1] We dig deeper. Carefully, we clear away the muck to reveal the silver gleam of a large and crumpled piece of machinery.

The Villagers of Yakeyama and Kyōgase

What country village, faced with the wrath of an occupying army, would not have sought to protect their friends and loved ones? Now that the dust has settled over the last sixty years, some communities in Japan, such as the recent case in Mebari City of Mie Prefecture, show that people do have the courage to face up to those days. At a local Buddhist temple they have erected a monument to the eleven crewmen of a B-29 that was shot down on June 6, 1945, after a bombing mission to Kobe. The residents there are forthright about the fact that they caught and killed at least nine of the crewmen. The older ones who remember the incident bring their grandchildren to the site, tell them what happened, and urge them not to repeat the same mistakes.[2] Many in the West are either unaware or unimpressed by these places of quiet reconciliation, but there exist across rural Japan many who not only admit the shame of their country's wartime past, they regret what happened and try to make amends on a personal level. In their temples they pray for the souls of the dead and leave flowers. They sit solemnly and thoughtfully as their priests offer somber mantras for the souls of the American airmen who died in their midst. As the smoke of the fragrant incense fills the air, they contemplate the ashes of the American soldiers, some of which are still kept within the temple, and of how they are now mingled with the ashes of the Japanese civilians they killed during the bombing raids. In death, they sleep together while Japanese of conscience go forth to emphasize 'peace education' (heiwa kyōiku) in an effort to create a better society.

Little of this has reached the villagers of former Yakeyama and Kyōgase. The price of silence has been high and the weight of old secrets grows heavier with each passing year. Not a week goes by when the elderly do not look at that field and remember.[3] The fields and lives of the villagers of Yakeyama have been inextricably linked for many generations. Although stillness returned to the village, peace was more elusive. In the same way as their fields, the toxic waste of hidden shame still lies buried beneath the surface.

Villagers in Yakeyama remain convinced, after all, that if anyone had killed the crewmen, it would have been those folks over in Kyōgase. They were the first to make contact with the crewmen. They are the ones who to this day refuse to talk about what happened. It was there that the stories of torture and death had started. But it was the people of Yakeyama who had been left to clean up the mess and endure the persecution of American War Crimes investigators. Keiichi Meguro was hailed as a local hero for his part in saving the village and for taking the brunt of the American investigators' interrogations. But his health suffered as a result of the ordeal. In his later years his wife fiercely protected her husband from historians and others who wanted to discover what he really knew.[4] 'I don't want to remember those days,' she once said, and as an afterthought, 'there shouldn't be any more wars.'[5] Such words are echoed in Kyōgase, but even Japanese researchers who have studied the incident of the

150

Jordan Crew have been sent packing when discovered asking questions about this taboo subject.[6] In my own experience from this research, I have found that those who have the least to say about such events are sometimes those who have the most to tell.

The majority of those who participated in the events of July 20 lived long lives, tilled the tortured soil and raised their families. When I interviewed them in Yakeyama, their main concern was that young people today eat less rice than before, opting instead for bread. The meaning was clear – now our grandchildren eat bread just like those fliers we buried long ago. We and our rice are rejected. We are passing away, and so is our way of life.

The Jordan Crew

Little is known about what happened to Gordon Jordan after he left the military in 1946, with the rank of Major. It is unknown as to whether he ever came to terms with his ultimate responsibility as the air commander for the events that took place on the last mission over Niigata. His former crewmen hesitated to speak much about Jordan's life following the war. Some hinted about a long battle with alcoholism. There were whispers of disbelief concerning a story about him flying planes in South America without a license. Others spoke of a story they heard that, later in life, Jordan had become a Christian evangelist. None of these stories changed the fierce loyalty and enduring respect that his former crewmen felt for Jordan. If anything, their love for 'Porky', as they referred to him, only seemed grow over the years. They have chosen to remember him as he was during those fleeting days in 1945. My repeated attempts to find his family in order fill in the gaps of his life were unsuccessful. Even Jordan's death was mysterious. Files at the US Department of Veteran Affairs state that he died in the mid 1970s, though records at the 6th Bomb Group say he died in 1996. Burkle died when he was only in his 40s. Some, such as Garin and Grant, went on to become successful businessmen. Others, such as Dickerson and McGraw, made a career of the Air Force.

Trump finished college and went to seminary, but was drafted during the Korean War. There was again the need for experienced B-29 crewmen. On his first day, Trump told his commanding officer about his ordeal in Japan. Soon afterwards he was transferred to a base in Alaska for the duration of the war.[7] This probably saved Trump's life, since B-29s were woefully outclassed by the new Soviet MiG-15 jet fighters flown by the North Koreans.[8] Trump continued to serve for several years as an Air Force chaplain and then for many more as a successful Lutheran minister in Pennsylvania. But the memories of his role in bombing Japanese civilians, his decision that night over Niigata and those days in the prison of the *kempei-tai* became his personal 'thorn in the flesh' throughout his many years of service to others.

Some Christians gravitate towards the stories of believers who overcame great suffering during times of war. But for every account of a Corrie ten Boom, there are many more like Trump's that go unnoticed. They are overlooked because they fail to depict the preferred picture, that of a saint overcoming all manner of evil. The glare of fragile humanity is too stark to bear. However, Trump's time in Tokyo was a poignant reminder to Christians that even more than the life of Christ, sometimes it is the life Saint Peter that can become the model for their spiritual development. Like Peter, Paul Trump was inexperienced in combat, frightened in the face of persecution, and misunderstood by those closest to him. Perhaps as a result of these experiences he was able to minister in the churches where he served with gentle understanding. Trump's contribution to his community as a man of peace was, in my estimation, far greater than anything he could have done as a man of war. As he walked this path Trump learned that, at the end of the day, there is grace after all.

Each crewman took different paths in their attempt to deal with the memories of their capture and imprisonment. Those who stayed in the military had a support system of sorts from those who had had similar experiences, and who could show their understanding in ways that would not cause discomfort to a rough, blue collar man. Some became increasingly bitter as the years went on and harbored a dark place in their lives that was disturbing to friends and family members. Others, such as Wiernik, tried to forget the whole affair and move forward. None of these approaches did much to alleviate the chilling nightmares and crushing bouts of depression which have pursued them even into old age. Little could assuage the thoughts about those who did not return home, or why.

> I remember being at home one night, and there's a bed that I could have slept in, but it was too soft; I slept on the floor. I was used to sleeping on a wooden floor [in the *kempei-tai* prison]. And I was on this floor, thinking about everything that had happened, and wondering, and the thought came to me, 'Why am I alive, when friends of mine are obviously dead?' I thought, 'How can I...join my friends?' And there was only one way, and I remembered that gun I had left behind. So I briefly entertained suicide, to join my friends, and it actually was to join my friends. But of course [the thought] was rejected almost immediately, but the thought did enter my head. The other thought, 'Why am I alive?' That is a very difficult question, because some people say, 'God has saved you.' Well, why didn't he save the others? So you get these questions, and 'No, you're alive because you are going to do something great.' Well, you are dead because you do nothing great?[9]

Only a few, such as McGraw and Trump, came to a point in their lives where they could move past the pain and put themselves in the place of their captors. It was then that they learned to let their former enemies off the hook – to truly forgive. Trump once said,

> I'm grateful that the Japanese civilians there didn't have guns, otherwise, we'd all have been killed. It was war. If the same thing had happened in Lancaster County [Pennsylvania]...if a Japanese plane had gone down there, and with most of the farmers out here with deer rifles, well, I imagine the bodies of those fellows would have been so riddled with bullets that by the time the police got there you wouldn't be able to identify the bodies.[10]

Trump's admission is that ordinary people are capable of extraordinary acts of cruelty during a war. What are labeled as atrocities after the fact are the acts that are often committed by the boy or girl next door. They do terrible things during wartime, not because they were particularly brutal in their temperament, but because their virtues and devotion had been co-opted by political forces larger than their own small dreams. Elites and their ideologies had induced them to pour their lives down the twisted drain of whatever national interest, holy war, or regional conflict happened to be pressing at the time. Intoxicated by the burning drink of nationalism, few were able to avoid the inevitable slide into darkness. In the end, they find themselves in the company of LeMay. They justify their actions by pronouncing, 'all war is immoral.'[11]

The Struggle for an Honorable Legacy

At the completion of my final interview with Trump, I had said my goodbyes and turned to leave, when suddenly he took my hand, looked deeply into my eyes, and with the silent, compelling force of some august forebear who had come back from the other side, commanded: 'Don't go making us out to be some sort of heroes.' Garin wrote much the same, urging that this book not gloss over any of the unpleasant details, 'History is only written in truths or else it is propaganda.'[12] Nevertheless, throughout the writing of this book there was a constant tension between how the villagers of Yakeyama and the Jordan Crew wanted to be remembered, what they did, and what can be known. The truth, if it can be discovered at all, floats furtively within these confines.

In telling their stories, the villagers often wished to divert the focus to their hunger, or the story of how one soldier from the anti-aircraft crew near Niitsu had fallen in love with a local girl and settled down in the area. They told stories about the Korean slave laborer who had escaped a coal mine, and how the villagers had hidden him from the authorities while they fed him and taught him Japanese.[13] They spoke of the times when they collected food to be taken to Niigata POW Camp 5B.[14] In their indirect, but evocative style of communication, the message was clear. 'We are not monsters. We are ordinary people. What happened on July 20, 1945 was one summer night in the heat of the moment – one night of violence in a thousand years of quiet history. See us for who we are – farmers. We grow rice. We help others when we can. Look at our years of labor, our joyful harvest festivals, and our peaceful rites of passage. This is who we really are.'

Most of the Jordan Crew, in their more lucid moments, seemed to understand these sentiments. They too came from rural communities and knew something of what the rules of engagement would have been had the shoe been on the other foot. The source of many of their bitter memories might be expressed as, 'Maybe we had it coming, but we were there when you beat and starved us...you enjoyed it too much. All we'd like is an apology.'

In a manner remarkably similar to the villagers of Yakeyama, at their core, the members of the Jordan Crew I spoke with also wanted to be remembered sympathetically. Their implicit message was equally clear. 'We were not murderers. We were ordinary men following orders. We feel bad for the fire-bombings, but there wasn't anything we could do about it. We were scared, and didn't want to be out there, but we had a job to do and we did our best for our country.'

Unfortunately it is at this point where the compassion ends. Most of the Japanese that I spoke with during the writing of this book expressed silent but burning indignation upon hearing these words. For them, it is inconceivable, even arrogant, that soldiers, after bombing women and children and after burning entire cities to the ground, could then throw up their arms in surrender and expect humane treatment as a POW. If I were to summarize their responses to the Jordan Crew, it would be, 'maybe you were following orders, and if we had been in your situation, we would have probably done the same thing. Be grateful that you only got away with a beating. And, by the way, no apologies.'

Those of us who are younger might yearn for reconciliation, if not for their sake, for ours. But except for those miraculous moments when a few individuals have crossed to the other side in an effort to make peace (and as a result, to find healing), there is little hope for reconciliation with the majority of this generation who are still with us. Too much time has passed. They are too old. They are too set in their ways. For them, it is too late. They have carried this burden long enough. We should let them pass.

In the beginning of this book, I wrote that there are no heroes in this story – only survivors. If there are any villains, these would be the decision makers on both sides of the war. They were the ones who had whipped their tribes into a frenzy, who had inflamed the ignorance of simple country folk with racist rhetoric and then threw them together into a dark, muddy field late at night. Those in the business of war justify doing this to their people. Robert McNamara, looking back over those days, felt convinced that what he and others did to the ordinary people in this story was necessary in order to secure a greater good.

> How much evil must we do in order to do good? We have certain ideals, certain responsibilities. Recognize that at times you will have to engage in evil, but minimize it. I remember reading that General Sherman in the Civil War – the mayor of Atlanta pleaded with him to save the city. And Sherman essentially said to the mayor just before he torched it and burned it down: 'War is cruel. War is cruelty.' That was the way LeMay felt. He was trying to save the country. He was trying to save our nation. And in the process, he was prepared to do whatever killing was necessary. It's a very, very difficult position for sensitive human beings to be in.[15]

And yet, is not sensitivity an important characteristic of what it means to be human, and to be humane? How much of our humanity must we sacrifice in order to preserve it? How much brutality must we engage in, in order to learn compassion? Most certainly, those who believe that war is necessary (or at least unavoidable) would counter these questions with the statement that military strength ensures peace and security. This is a strong argument which must be taken seriously, and yet I would quietly observe that military strength seems to invite as many wars as it prevents.

Regardless of where one falls in these debates, it cannot be denied that in the years following the Second World War, whatever else happened, the elite classes of both America and Japan have secured enormous gains, while those ordinary people, the ones who had wielded the weapons, have largely lost. Japan got its sphere of economic prosperity in Asia, America got its base in the East. The greater good had been secured, but only for the great. Former Allied POWs were dispossessed by their own governments, forbidden in 1951 by the Treaty of San Francisco from seeking compensation from Japan for their suffering. The work of the CIA to prop up Japan's privileged few as a bulwark against Communism meant that, in large measure, democracy never took hold in the country. Democracy, whatever it may mean to the Japanese people, became a bonsai – something quite beautiful to behold from a casual distance, but nevertheless, a fragile object which must be constantly trimmed and bound by multitudinous hands so that it is kept small and manageable. And after both sides of those who fought and sacrificed in that war listened to the obligatory platitudes of their great leaders, all were left to deal with scarred lives in solitude. Villagers and crewmen alike suffered deeply as a result of that war, and to a certain extent, so have the generations which have followed.

Six decades on, the age-old problems which plagued our world sixty years earlier still thrive – issues such as nationalism, tribalism and fundamentalism, the flames of which are fanned ever stronger by media-driven stereotypes and polarized war-mongering. The unresolved nature of the Second World War remains a festering wound in Asia. Especially since the first Gulf War in 1990, but even as early as the 1950s, the United States has been actively encouraging a more militaristic Japan to serve as the first line of defense against China and North Korea.[16] And in recent years, despite disturbing signs that Japan is returning to a more aggressive stance, the silence of the United States speaks volumes. Japanese nationalism is back in vogue. Prime Ministers stoke the coals of hatred by denying the Imperial government's involvement in the entrapment of local women for exploitation in military brothels, and by their visits to the Yasukuni Shrine, a war memorial that contains remains of the Japanese veterans of foreign wars and the ashes of several executed war criminals. These public displays of imperial affection are as offensive to Japan's Asian neighbors as the visit of an American president to a Confederate war memorial would be to African Americans. Old rivalries are being revived, with repeated pronouncements from government ministers and the Japanese media about the Chinese threat or the North Korean threat. Some government officials have even mentioned that Japan is not prohibited from making atomic weapons of its own before their handlers could sweep such gaffes under the rug.[17]

In February 2005, I attended a luncheon at the Foreign Correspondents Club in Tokyo for Yasuhiro Nakasone, a former prime minister known for his conservative political beliefs. Although officially in retirement, he continues to exert considerable influence over the Liberal Democratic Party as one of their elder statesmen. In his speech he talked of working to make Japan strong again, of seeing to it that Japan would be proud once more, and of fostering reforms that would make Japan a 'normal country.' Normal for Nakasone meant having an army that could participate fully in international peacekeeping missions. He spoke of the need to change Japan's pacifist constitution in order to make this dream a reality. Few of the reporters at my table believed that such changes would take place. But in the space of two years, Japan is on the brink of doing just that. The government has already enacted measures to consolidate the Self-Defense Forces into a newly-created Ministry of Defense which will make overseas missions a main part of its mandate. The remaining changes to Japan's constitution will soon follow.

Many of the university students I teach in Niigata echo the words of Nakasone and other conservative politicians. These students, who will be the future leaders of Japanese society, want Japan to become a country that is strong enough to hold its own in this post-9/11 world. I find such views disturbing, since I believe that Japan's ability to maintain a pacifist stance during the violence of the latter half of the 20th century was a sign of great strength. By renouncing war, Japan was an inspiring symbol of what a 'normal country' should truly be. It seems to me that those countries which habitually abandon peaceful dialogue in favor of military action are the aberration. These societies' inability to break the futile cycle of violence that has cursed humanity for millennia is a sign of their weakness, not strength.

Increasingly, the Japanese media in recent years portray Imperial Japan's last war as a tragic, twilight struggle against a remorseless, technologically advanced enemy. These are designed to influence Japanese youth who, because of the silence of their grandparents and the sanitized textbooks approved by an increasingly conservative Ministry of Education, know little about the horror of war. Recent changes to Japan's educational system have now required that 'patriotic education' be included as a part of the curriculum. Students must now be taught about what it means to love Japan, to have a public spirit and to maintain tradition. This comes at a time when Tokyo's governor has fired or severely punished scores of teachers for not participating in the singing of Japan's national anthem during special ceremonies – an anthem which is a song of praise to the Divine Emperor. Thus it is not surprising that some of my own college students, in moments of inebriation, have spoken of wanting to go to North Korea in order to fight and die for the Emperor.

Such sentiments will certainly find their counterpart among drunken rural Americans who howl for the South to rise again, and it is easy to discount the ravings of this lunatic fringe. More difficult to ignore, however, are the attitudes of the average members of the younger generations who have been taught to view the Second World War solely in terms of a victim's history. As well, many, if not most in Anglo-American countries, if they think of this war at all, will speak it in terms of a Hollywood portrayal of military victories. Both views in my opinion are distorted caricatures of history.

For Anglo-American youths, it is important that they understand that, for every soldier who raises a flag in triumph over distant battlefields, there are the thousands of others who die alone and forlorn in the darkness, crying in pain as the life is hacked and beaten out of them. This too is the price of victory. For the Japanese youth who view this war in terms of suffering and victimization, they must face the fact that the suffering was not theirs, and that those who are on the losing side of a war are often the most vicious. To defile dead bodies in rage, to starve and torture captives – these too are the things that victims do, just before the end. For the sake of the young in all of these countries, it is necessary to go backwards, to pierce the present shame and look full in the face of those dark war years. It is important to understand what war does to a person and to understand how governments exploit the poor at these times. It is essential that they know that, after having outlived their usefulness, ordinary people will be, as they have always been, discarded and forgotten. It is vital for younger generations to learn that before one takes up arms to fight for God and Country, they need to know the difference.

Fragment of Jordan's B-29 as it is taken to the Yokogōshi Municipal History Department

Together, we struggled to place the large piece of wreckage from Jordan's B-29 into the back of a truck. A poignant symbol of the futility of war, it would be cleaned up and put on display during an autumn festival at the Yokogōshi Community Center. There, a few children would ask about it. Even fewer old timers, who would look at the ugly lump of metal, would answer with leaden voices. Every year, a few more of those who remember those days are gone. And yet, it will not be forgotten, that Field of Spears.

The question is, however, will we remember its lessons?

[1] Chozo Shimizu, interview by Toshihide Uemura, July 1, 1998, tape recording, The B-29 Downing Incident (B29 撃墜事件について), Former Yokogōshi City History Department, Yokogōshi, Niigata.

[2] Go Kumagai, 'Monument Erected to Mourn and Comfort the Souls of 11 B-29 Crewmen in Mebari, Mie Prefecture (追悼碑撃墜Ｂ２９爆撃機の米兵１１人を慰霊　三重・名張),' *Asahi Shinbun Online/Yahoo News*, May 28 2006, Society Section. http://headlines.yahoo.co.jp/hl?a=20060528-00000007-maip-soci/ (accessed June 9, 2006).

[3] Motoichi Fujita, Tadashi Saito, Hikaru Sato, interview by author, January 16, 2004, MD Recording.

[4] 佐藤貞太郎 (Teitaro Sato), 'B-29 撃墜余談 (Digressions about the B-29 Downing),' *五頭郷土文化 (Gozu Hometown Culture)* 7 (December, 1984), 64.

[5] 'American soldiers surrounded by spear-wielding villagers (竹やりの村民米兵囲む),' *Niigata Nippo*, August 12 2000.

[6] Anonymous B, interview by author, June 20, 2003, notes.

[7] Paul Trump, interview by author, March 23, 2004, MD Recording.

[8] Daniel T. Kuehl, 'Refighting the Last War: Electronic Warfare and U.S. Air Force B-29 Operations in the Korean War, 1950-1953,' *The Journal of Military History* 56, no. 1 (January 1992), 87-112.

[9] Robert Michelson, interview by Saylor, Thomas (Apple Valley, Minnesota, November 2, 2001), *Prisoner of War Oral History Project: World War Two and Korea* (2001-2002), http://people.csp.edu/saylor/POWproject/POWinterviews/MichelsonR.htm. (accessed February 7, 2006).

[10] Paul Trump, March 23, 2004.

[11] Richard Rhodes, 'LeMay's Vision of War,' interview by PBS Online. *The American Experience: The Race for the Superbomb*. http://www.pbs.org/wgbh/amex/bomb/filmmore/reference/interview/rhodes07.html. (accessed May 10, 2005).

[12] Milton Garin, e-mail message to author, May 26, 2005.

[13] Chuzo Sato, Yoshio Ito and Miyo Meguro, interview by Toshihide Uemura, July 1, 1998, tape recording, The B-29 Downing Incident (B29 撃墜事件について), Former Yokogōshi City History Department, Yokogōshi, Niigata.

[14] Motoichi Fujita, Tadashi Saito, Hikaru Sato, January 16, 2004.

[15] *Fog of War - Eleven Lessons from the Life of Robert S. McNamara*, DVD, dir. Errol Morris, 107 min. (New York: Sony Pictures Classics, 2003).

[16] Eric Johnston, 'U.S. Looks to Expand Japan's Military Role,' *The Japan Times*, May 2, 2004, http://www.japantimes.co.jp/cgi-bin/getarticle.pl5?nn20040502a1.htm. (accessed January 1, 2006). 'U.S. Used Japan's Gulf War Isolation to Push it onto World Stage,' *The Japan Times*, December 18 2005, http://www.japantimes.co.jp/cgi-bin/getarticle.pl5?nn20051218a3.htm. (accessed January 1, 2005).

[17] Kenji Hall, 'Japan's A-Bomb Goal Still Long Way Off in '45,' *The Japan Times*, March 7, 2003, http://www.japantimes.com/cgi-bin/makeprfy.pl5?nn20030307b7.htm. (accessed September 19, 2005).

INDEX

159